THE KASHMIR FILES

KASHMIRI PANDITS

MR VIVEK KUMAR PANDEY

Made with ♥ on the Notion Press Platform
www.notionpress.com

Contents

Foreword

In This Book There Is Complete Story Of Kashmir Files & Exodus of Kashmiri Hindus, Kashmiri Pandits.During Writing This Book No Character, No Religion & No Caste Are Harmed. It's Only For Study Purpose. We don't want to hurt anyone.

Preface

Author biography in English :

MY NAME IS VIVEK KUMAR PANDEY . I WAS BORN IN 30 SEP 2002,I AM FROM SURAT GUJARAT INDIA.MY DREAM WAS TO BE GOOD WRITERS ,MY FAMILY SUPPORTED ME TO SUCCESSFUL AND I CAN DO IT MY SELF.How do I write? That is a question, I believe, that can be honestly answered by me."CELEBRATING YOUNGEST WRITER AWARD WINNER IN GUJARAT 1ST RANK" MR PANDEY JI . I may think I did a good job writing something. The reader is the one who decides the quality of my writing. I do find writing to be natural to me and therefore find it to be a real challenge. My trick as a challenged writer is to do the best I can and know that I am happy with the final outcome. It may take a while to do my best and there may be quite a few problems I run into along the way.

I am not a greedy person those who are thinking about me and my self I never tried it anyone people suffering from sadness ,I trying to get promoted people suffering from happiness and joy in your Life Time. Now in current situation in India and also world people are unemployed and have no many but our indian governor help to people to get free food from ration card , i also take part in leadership team ,i am Motivational speaker , Film script writer. There was my two dream firstly writer and secondly actor & also my own film is upcoming soon i done almost completely completed script for my film .I AM GOING TO SAY WORD OF HEART TOUCH OUT PLEASE READ IT" , firstly i thanks my father he supports me in this field they always getting inspired me by own his words and behavior ,they always said that he was a biggest person in the world in future and also they purchase fruit and chocolate for me in anytime & anyway , firstly my father buy him then call me Vivek you want a chocolate i will say yes papa but how many tell me ,papa: you tell me how much i buy him i told 1 or 2 chocolate but my father purchase whole the boxes of chocolate and they get suprised me.

MY FATHER WAS BORN IN " 20 SEPTEMBER" 1971 IN INDIA.

1) MY FATHER FAVORITE CLOTHES IS KURTA PAIJMA AND ALSO STYLES SHOE

2) FAVORITE SINGER IS KISHORE DA

3) FAVORITE STATE GUJARAT AND KOLKATA , HIS VILLAGE IN BIHAR

4) FAVORITE COLOR BLACK AND WHITE

THEY ALSO LOVE cricket like IPL and one day t-20 .they also like watching a News daily and heard the song daily ,they also interested in tik tok video but in current time tik tok is banned in india but also few videos are in you tube. In lockdown time my family and me very enjoy day daily. my father play daily ludo with his sister and son, daughter.they always loved tea and coffee anytime call me . I make it tea for my father but some reason after the April to june they are suffering from fever and cough , weakness on 6 June 2020 my father death. they not told me say bye bye his life. After death of 6 June on 10 june my mom and dad anniversary.but my father is Best in the world they can do anything for me please take care of father and respect it of your parents.

ONE
KASHMIRI PANDITS

- **Kashmiri Pandits**

1. During Writing This Book No Character, No Religion & No Caste Are Harmed. It's Only For Study Purpose. We don't want to hurt anyone.

The Kashmiri Pandits also known as Kashmiri Brahmins are a group of Kashmiri Hindus and a part of the larger Saraswat Brahmin community of India. They belong to the Pancha Gauda Brahmin group from the Kashmir Valley, a mountainous region located within the Indian union territory of Jammu and Kashmir. Kashmiri Pandits are Hindu Kashmiris native to the Kashmir Valley, and the only remaining Hindu Kashmiris after the large-scale of conversion of the Valley's population to Islam during the medieval times. Prompted by the growth of Islamic militancy in the valley, large numbers left in the exodus of the 1990s. Even so, small numbers remain.

- **History of Kashmir**

The Hindu caste system of the Kashmir region was influenced by the influx of Buddhism from the time of Asoka, around the third century BCE, and a consequence of this was that the traditional lines of varna were blurred, with the exception of that for the Brahmins. Another notable feature of early Kashmiri society was the relative high regard in which women were held when compared to their position in other communities of the period.

A historically contested region, Northern India was subject to attack from Turkic and Arab regimes from the eighth century onwards, but they generally ignored the mountain-circled Kashmir Valley in favour of easier pickings elsewhere. It was not until the fourteenth century that Muslim rule was finally established in the Valley and when this happened it did not occur primarily as a consequence of invasion so much as because of internal problems resulting from the weak rule and corruption endemic in the Hindu Lohara dynasty. Mohibbul Hasan describes this collapse as

The Dãmaras grew powerful, defied royal authority, and by their constant revolts plunged the country into confusion. Life and property were not safe, agriculture declined, and there were periods when trade came to a standstill. Socially and morally too the court and the country had sunk to the depths of degradations.

The Brahmins had something to be particularly unhappy about during the reign of the last Lohara king, for Sũhadeva chose to include them in his system of onerous taxation, whereas previously they appear to have been exempted.

- **Kashmir Medieval history**

Zulju, who was probably a Mongol from Turkistan, wreaked devastation in 1320, when he commanded a force that conquered many regions of the Kashmir Valley. However, Zulju was probably not a Muslim. The actions of Sultan Sikandar Butshikan (1389–1413), the seventh Muslim ruler in Kashmir were also significant to the area. The Sultan has been referred to as an iconoclast because of his destruction of many non-Muslim religious symbols and the manner in which he forced the population to convert or flee. Many followers of the traditional religions who did not convert to Islam instead migrated to other parts of India.

The migrants included some Pandits, although it is possible that some of this community relocated for economic reasons as much as to escape the new rulers. Brahmins were at that time generally being offered grants of land in other areas by rulers seeking to utilise the traditionally high literacy and general education of the community, as well as the legitimacy conferred upon them by association. The outcome of this shift both in population and in religion was that the Kashmir Valley became a predominantly Muslim region. It was during the 14th century that the Kashmiri Pandits likely split into their three subcastes: Guru/Bāchabat , Jotish, and Kārkun (who were historically mainly employed by the government). The majority of Kashmiri Brahmins are Kārkuns, and this is likely due to the conversion of the majority of Kashmiris to Islam, which led to a decrease in demand for Hindu priests, which led most Kashmiri Brahmins to seek secular employment.

Butshikan's heir, the devout Muslim Zain-ul-Abidin (1423–74), was tolerant of Hindus to the extent of sanctioning a return to Hinduism of those who had been forcibly converted to the Muslim faith, as well as becoming involved in the restoration of temples. He respected the learning of these Pandits, to whom he gave land as well as encouraging those who had left to return. He operated a meritocracy and both Brahmins and Buddhists were among his closest advisors.

- **Kashmir Modern history**

D.L. Sheth, the former director of the Center for the Study of Developing Societies in India (CSDS), lists Indian communities that constituted the middle class and were traditionally "Urban and professional" (following professions like doctors, lawyers, teachers, engineers, etc.) immediately after Independence in 1947. This list included the Kashmiri Pandits, the Nagar Brahmins from Gujarat; the South Indian Brahmins; the Punjabi Khatris, and Kayasthas from northern India; Chitpawans and CKPs (Chandraseniya

Kayastha Prabhus) from Maharashtra; the Probasi and the Bhadralok Bengalis; the Parsis and the upper crusts of Muslim and Christian communities. According to P.K.Verma, "Education was a common thread that bound together this pan Indian elite" and almost all the members of these communities could read and write English and were educated beyond school.

- **Exodus of Kashmiri Hindus**

The Kashmiri Pandits had been a favoured section of the population of the valley during Dogra rule (1846–1947). 20 per cent of them left the valley as a consequence of the 1950 land reforms,and by 1981 the Pandit population amounted to 5 per cent of the total.

- **An artpiece of three Kashmiri Pandit women**

They began to leave in much greater numbers in the 1990s during the eruption of militancy, following persecution and threats by radical Islamists and militants. The events of 19 January 1990 were particularly vicious. On that day, mosques issued declarations that the Kashmiri Pandits were Kafirs and that the males had to leave Kashmir, convert to Islam or be killed. Those who chose to the first of these were told to leave their women behind. The Kashmiri Muslims were instructed to identify Pandit homes so they could be systematically targeted for conversion or killing.

According to a number of authors, approximately 100,000 of the total Kashmiri Pandit population of 140,000 left the valley during the 1990s. Other authors have suggested a higher figure for the exodus, ranging from the entire population of over 150,000, to 190,000 of a total Pandit population of 200,000, to a number as high as 800,000. The nature of the planned exodus has remain controversial, with the involvement of then Governor Jagmohan in organising a clandestine exodus been a subject of controversy. Many of the refugee Kashmiri Pandits have been living in abject conditions in refugee camps of Jammu. The government has reported on the terrorist threats to Pandits still living in the Kashmir region.

Some Hindus across India tried to help the Pandits. Bal Thackeray from Maharashtra got seats reserved in engineering colleges for the children of these Pandits. He was one of the first persons to help them after which Punjab also followed suit.

In 2009 the Oregon Legislative Assembly passed a resolution to recognise 14 September 2007, as Martyrs Day to acknowledge ethnic cleansing and campaigns of terror inflicted on non-Muslim minorities of Jammu and Kashmir by terrorists seeking to establish an Islamic state.

In 2010, the Government of Jammu and Kashmir noted that 808 Pandit families, comprising 3,445 people, were still living in the Valley and that financial and other incentives put in place to encourage others to return there had been unsuccessful. According to a J&K government report, 219 members of the community had been killed in the region between 1989 and 2004 but none thereafter. The local organisation of pandits in Kashmir, Kashmir Pandit Sangharsh Samiti after carrying out a survey in 2008 and 2009, said that 399 Kashmiri Pandits were killed by insurgents from 1990 to 2011 with 75% of them being killed during the first year of the Kashmiri insurgency.

The exiled community had hoped to return after the situation improved. They have not done so because the situation in the Valley remains unstable and they fear a risk to their lives.

As of October 2015, only 1 Kashmiri Pandit family returned to the Kashmir valley since 1990 according to the Jammu & Kashmir government despite the financial assistance being given for rehabilitation. As of 2016, a total of 1,800 Kashmiri Pandit youths have returned to the valley since the announcing of Rs. 1,168-crore package in 2008 by the UPA government.

- **Jammu Kashmir Liberation Front**

There are zones set up with offices for relief.Many Orders, Circulars and recommendations have been issued for relief of Kashmiri Pandits.The Jammu And Kashmir Migrant Immovable Property (Preservation, Protection And Restraint on Distress Sales) Act, 1997, provides that "Any person who is an unauthorised occupant or recipient of any usufruct of any immovable property of the migrant shall pay to the migrant such compensation for the period of unauthorised occupation and in such a manner as may be determined by the District Magistrate."

- **Jammu and Kashmir Reorganisation Act, 2019**

Following the migration of the Kashmiri Pandit community, various socio-political organisations have sprung up to represent the cause of the displaced community. The most prominent among these are the All India Kashmiri Samaj or AIKS, All India Kashmiri Pandit conference, Panun Kashmir & Kashmiri Samiti. These organisations are involved in rehabilitation of the community in the valley through peace negotiations, mobilisation of human rights groups and job creation for the Pandits.

Panun Kashmir has made demands for a separate homeland for the community in the southern part of Kashmir. Ikkjutt Jammu, a political party in Jammu and Kashmir, advocates for two Union Territories in Kashmir, one being Panun Kashmir for Kashmiri Hindus.

- **Kashmiri couple getting married in a traditional ceremony at Jammu**

According to the 1941 census, there were 78,800 Kashmiri Pandits in the Kashmir Valley. They were distributed into the two districts of Valley, the Baramulla district, where Hindus constituted 2.1 percent of the population; 12,919 Hindus out of 612,428 total. and the Anantnag district, where they were 7.84 percent of the population.

Scholar Christopher Snedden states that the Pandits made up about 6 per cent of the Kashmir Valley's population in 1947. By 1950, their population declined to 5 per cent as many Pandits moved to other parts of India due to the uncompensated land redistribution policy, the unsettled nature of Kashmir's accession to India and the threat of economic and social decline.

In the 1981 census, the Kashmir Division had 124,078 Hindus, the majority of whom were Pandits. Scholar Alexander Evans estimates by 1990, there would have been 160,000–170,000 Pandits in the Kashmir Valley. Following the 1989 insurgency, a great majority of Pandits felt threatened and left the Kashmir Valley for other parts of India. A large number settled in the Jammu Division of the State and the National Capital Region of India. Some emigrated to other countries entirely. By 2011, only an estimated 2,700-3,400 Pandits remained in the Kashmir Valley.

According to Indian government, more than 60,000 families are registered as Kashmiri migrants including some Sikh and Muslim families. Most families were resettled in Jammu, NCR and other neighbouring states.

- **Sharda Peeth**

Kashmir has also been a land of Sun worship with shrines such as Martand Sun Temple established by Lalitaditya Muktapida. Sun worship is believed to have been brought into Kashmir by Kushan kings from Iran. Lalitaditya's predecessor, Ranaditya, is said to have built the first sun temple. Wanvun singing is an integral part of Kashmiri Pandit religious ceremonies.

- **Mount Harmukh**

Harmukh is traditionally revered by Kashmiri Pandits and in 2009 there was an attempt by them to revive pilgrimages to the site. The Mata Kheerbhawani temple shrine in Srinagar, considered one of the holiest Hindu shrines, saw the largest gathering of Kashmiri

Pandits in the Kashmir valley in 2012.The shrine is located in Tullamulla village, 24 km from Srinagar in Ganderbal district.

- **Kashmiri Pandit Festivals**

The Kashmiri Pandits festivals include Shivratri (or Herath in the Kashmiri language) which is one of the major festivals of Kashmiri Pandits. Navreh or the Kashmiri lunar new year is also an important Pandit festival.

- **Kashmir Culture & Dress**

Kshemendra's detailed records from the eleventh century describe many items of which the precise nature is unknown. It is clear that tunics known as kanchuka were worn long-sleeved by men and in both long- and half-sleeved versions by women. Caps were worn, as well as a type of turban referred to as a shirahshata, while footwear consisted of leather shoes and boots, worn with socks. Some items were elaborate, such as the peacock shoes – known as mayuropanah – worn by followers of fashion, and steel-soled shoes adorned with floral designs, lubricated internally with beeswax. They also wear the mekhalā, which is a type of girdle.

There are many references to the wearing of jewellery by both sexes, but a significant omission from them is any record of the dejihor worn on the ear by women today as a symbol of their being married. Kaw has speculated that this item of jewellery may not have existed at the time. The texts also refer to both sexes using cosmetics, and to the women adopting elaborate hairstyles. Men, too, might adopt stylish arrangements and wear flowers in their hair, if they had the financial means to do so.

- **Kashmir ancient traditional Music**

Henzae is an ancient traditional form of singing practised by Kashmiri Pandits at their festivals. It appears to have archaic features that suggest it is the oldest form of Kashmiri folk singing.

The Kashmiri Pandits have a tradition of consuming meat, including mutton and fish, but they obey restrictions laid down by the shastras of not eating the meat of forbidden animals such as beef and pork. Frederick J. Simoons says that according to some reports, Kashmiri Pandits also consume fish as part of their diet.

- **Kashmir Subcastes**

The Kashmiri Pandits are divided into three subcastes, Guru/ Bāchabat (priests), Jotish (astrologers), and Kārkun (who were historically mainly employed by the government). All three subcastes interdine and interteach, but only the Jotish and Kārkun subcastes intermarry.

TWO

EXODUS OF KASHMIRI HINDUS

- **Exodus of Kashmiri Hindus**

30–80 Kashmiri Pandits had been killed by insurgents by mid-year 1990 when the exodus was largely complete, according to several scholars. Indian Home Ministry data records 217 Hindus civilians fatalities during the four-year period, 1988 to 1991 another scholar estimates 228 Pandit civilian fatalities. Government of Jammu and Kashmir recorded 219 Pandit fatalities between 1989 and 2004.

The Exodus of Kashmiri Hindus, or Pandits, is their early-1990 migration, or flight, from the Muslim-majority Kashmir valley in Indian-administered Kashmir following rising violence in an insurgency. Of a total Pandit population of 120,000–140,000 some 90,000–100,000 left the valley or felt compelled to leave, and about 30 were killed. During the period of substantial migration, the insurgency was being led by a group calling for a secular and independent Kashmir, but there were also growing Islamist factions envisioning an Islamic state.

Although their numbers of dead and injured were low, the Pandits, who believed that Kashmir's culture was tied to India's, experienced fear and panic set off by targeted killings of some high-profile officials among their ranks and public calls for independence among the insurgents. The accompanying rumours and uncertainty together with the absence of guarantees for their safety by India's federal government might have been the latent causes of the exodus. The descriptions of the violence as "genocide" or "ethnic cleansing" in some Hindu nationalist publications or among suspicions voiced by some exiled Pandits are widely considered inaccurate, aggressive, or propaganda by scholars.

The Kashmir Valley, which is a part of the larger Kashmir region that has been the subject of a dispute between India and Pakistan from 1947, has been administered by India from approximately the same time. Before 1947, during the period of British Raj in India when Jammu and Kashmir was a princely state, Kashmiri Pandits, or Kashmiri Hindus, had stably constituted between 4% and 6% of the population of the Kashmir valley in censuses from 1889 to 1941; the remaining 94 to 95% of the population was Kashmiri Muslim.

By 1950, a large number of Pandits—whose elite owned over 30% of the arable land in the Valley—moved to other parts of India in the face of land reforms planned by the incoming administration of Sheikh Abdullah, the threat of socio-economic decline, and the unsettled nature of Kashmir's accession to India. In 1989 a persisting insurgency began in Kashmir. It was fed by Kashmiri dissatisfaction with India's federal government over rigging an assembly election in 1987 and disavowing a promise of greater autonomy. The dissatisfaction overflowed into an ill-defined uprising against the Indian state. The Jammu and Kashmir Liberation Front (JKLF), an organization that had generally secular antecedents and the predominant goal of political independence, led the uprising but did not abjure violence.

In early 1990, the vast majority of Kashmiri Hindus fled the valley in a mass-migration.More of them left in the following years so that, by 2011, only around 3,000 families remained. 30 or 32 Kashmiri Pandits had been killed by insurgents by mid-March 1990 when the exodus was largely complete, according to some scholars.

Indian Home Ministry data records 217 Hindu civilian fatalities during the four-year period, 1988 to 1991.

The reasons for this migration are vigorously contested. In 1989–1990, as calls by Kashmiri Muslims for independence from India gathered pace, many Kashmiri Pandits, who viewed self-determination to be anti-national, felt under pressure. The killings in the 1990s of a number of Pandit officials, may have shaken the community's sense of security, although it is thought some Pandits—by virtue of their evidence given later in Indian courts—may have acted as agents of the Indian state. The Pandits killed in targeted assassinations by the Jammu and Kashmir Liberation Front (JKLF) included some high-profile ones.

Occasional anti Hindu calls were made from mosques on loudspeakers asking Pandits to leave the valley. News of threatening letters created fear, though in later interviews the letters were seen to have been sparingly received. There were disparities between the accounts of the two communities, the Muslims and the Pandits. Many Kashmiri Pandits believed they were forced out of the Valley either by Pakistan and the militants it supported or the Kashmiri Muslims as a group.

Many Kashmiri Muslims did not support violence against religious minorities; the departure of the Kashmiri Pandits offered an excuse for casting Kashmiri Muslims as Islamic radicals, thereby contaminating their more genuine political grievances, and offering a rationale for their surveillance and violent treatment by the Indian state. Many Muslims in the Valley believed that the then Governor, Jagmohan had encouraged the Pandits to leave so as to have a free hand in more thoroughly pursuing reprisals against Muslims. Several scholarly views chalk the migration to genuine panic among the Pandits that stemmed as much from the religious vehemence among some of the insurgents as by the absence of guarantees for the Pandits' safety issued by the Governor.

Kashmiri Pandits initially moved to the Jammu Division, the southern half of Jammu and Kashmir, where they lived in refugee camps, sometimes in unkempt and unclean surroundings. At the time of their exodus, very few Pandits expected their exile to last beyond a few months. As the exile lasted longer, many displaced Pandits who were in the urban elite were able to find jobs in other parts of India, but those in the lower-middle-class, especially those from rural areas languished longer in refugee camps, with some living in poverty; this generated tensions with the host communities—whose social and religious practices, although Hindu, differed from those of the brahmin Pandits—and rendered assimilation more difficult.

Many displaced Pandits in the camps succumbed to emotional depression and a sense of helplessness. The cause of the Kashmiri Pandits was quickly championed by right-wing Hindu groups in India, which also preyed on their insecurities and further alienated them from Kashmiri Muslims. Some displaced Kashmiri Pandits have formed an organization called Panun Kashmir , which has asked for a separate homeland for Kashmiri Hindus in the Valley but has opposed autonomy for Kashmir on the grounds that it would promote the formation of an Islamic state. The return to the homeland in Kashmir also constitutes one of the main points of the ruling Bharatiya Janata Party's election platform. Kashmiri Pandits in exile have written autobiographical memoirs, novels, and poetry to record their experiences and to understand them. 19 January is observed by the Kashmiri Hindu communities as Exodus Day.

- **1986 Kashmir riots, Indira–Sheikh Accord, and Muslim United Front**

Under the 1975 Indira–Sheikh Accord, Sheikh Abdullah agreed to measures previously undertaken by the central government in Jammu and Kashmir to integrate the state into India. Farrukh Faheem, a sociologist at the University of Kashmir, states that it was met with hostility among the people of Kashmir and laid the groundwork for the future insurgency. Those opposed to the accords included Jamaat-e-Islami Kashmir, People's League in Indian Jammu and Kashmir, and the Jammu Kashmir Liberation

Front (JKLF) based in Pakistani-administered Azad Jammu and Kashmir. Since the mid-1970s, communalist rhetoric was being exploited in the state for votebank politics. Around this time, Pakistan's Inter-Services Intelligence (ISI) tried to spread Wahhabism in place of Sufism to foster religious unity within their nation, and the communalization aided their cause. Islamization of Kashmir began in the 1980s when Sheikh Abdullah's government changed the names of about 300 places to Islamic names. Sheikh also started delivering communal speeches in mosques that were similar to his confrontational pro-independence speeches in the 1930s. Additionally, he referred to Kashmiri Hindus as mukhbir , or informants of the Indian military.

The ISI's initial attempts to sow widespread unrest in Kashmir against the Indian administration were largely unsuccessful until the late-1980s. The American- and Pakistani-backed Afghan mujahideen's armed struggle against the Soviet Union in the Soviet–Afghan War, the Islamic Revolution in Iran and the Sikh insurgency in Indian Punjab against the Indian government became sources of inspiration for large numbers of Kashmiri Muslim youth.

Both the pro-independence JKLF and pro-Pakistan Islamist groups including Jamaat-e-Islami Kashmir mobilized the rapidly-growing anti-Indian sentiments amongst the Kashmiri population; the year of 1984 saw a pronounced rise in terrorist violence in Kashmir. Following the execution of JKLF militant Maqbool Bhat in February 1984, strikes and protests by Kashmiri nationalists broke out in the region, where large numbers of Kashmiri youth participated in widespread anti-India demonstrations and consequently faced heavy-handed reprisals by state security forces.

Critics of the then chief minister, Farooq Abdullah, charged him with losing control of the situation. His visit to Pakistani-administered Kashmir during this time became an embarrassment, where according to JKLF's Hashim Qureshi, he shared a platform with the JKLF. Abdullah asserted that he went on behalf of Indira Gandhi and his father, so that sentiments there could "be known first hand", although few people believed him. There were also allegations that he had allowed Khalistani militants to train in Jammu, although these were never proved to be true. On 2 July 1984, Ghulam Mohammad Shah, who had support from Indira Gandhi, replaced his brother-in-law Farooq Abdullah and assumed the role of chief minister after Abdullah was dismissed, in what was termed a "political coup".

G. M. Shah's administration, which did not have people's mandate, turned to Islamists and opponents of India, notably the Molvi Iftikhar Hussain Ansari, Mohammad Shafi Qureshi and Mohinuddin Salati, to gain some legitimacy through religious sentiments. This gave political space to Islamists who previously lost overwhelmingly in the 1983 state elections.

In 1986, Shah decided to construct a mosque within the premises of an ancient Hindu temple inside the New Civil Secretariat area in Jammu to be made available to the Muslim employees for 'Namaz'. People of Jammu took to streets to protest against this decision, which led to a Hindu-Muslim clash. In February 1986, Shah on his return to Kashmir valley retaliated and incited the Kashmiri Muslims by saying Islam Khatre Mein Hey

As a result, this led to the 1986 Kashmir riots where Kashmiri Hindus were targeted by the Kashmiri Muslims. Many incidents were reported in various areas where Kashmiri Hindus were killed and their properties and temples damaged or destroyed. The worst hit areas were mainly in South Kashmir and Sopore. During the Anantnag riot in February 1986, although no Hindu was killed, many houses and other properties belonging to Hindus were looted, burnt or damaged. An investigation of Anantnag riots revealed that members of the 'secular parties' in the state, rather than the Islamists, had played a key role in organising the violence to gain political mileage through religious sentiments. Shah called in the army to curb the violence, but it had little effect. His government was dismissed on 12 March 1986, by Governor Jagmohan following communal riots in south Kashmir, and led to Governor's rule in the state. The political fight was hence being portrayed as a conflict between "Hindu" New Delhi (Central Government), and its efforts to impose its will in the state, and "Muslim" Kashmir, represented by political Islamists and clerics.

For the 1987 state elections, various Islamist groups, including Jamaat-e-Islami Kashmir, organised themselves under the banner of Muslim United Front, with a manifesto to work for Islamic unity and against political interference from the centre. The two mainstrain parties (NC and INC) were allied together and won the election, However, the elections are widely believed to have been rigged in favour of the mainstream alliance and thus the government formed by Farooq Abdullah lacked legitimacy.

The corruption and alleged electoral malpractices were the catalysts for an insurgency. The Kashmiri militants killed anyone who openly expressed pro-India policies. Kashmiri Hindus were targeted specifically because they were seen as presenting Indian presence in Kashmir because of their faith. Though the insurgency had been launched by JKLF, groups rose over the next few months advocating for establishment of Nizam-e-Mustafa on Islamist groups proclaimed the Islamicisation of socio-political and economic set-up, merger with Pakistan, unification of ummah and establishment of an Islamic Caliphate. Liquidation of central government officials, Hindus, liberal and nationalist intellectuals, social and cultural activists was described as necessary to rid the valley of un-Islamic elements.

The relations among the mainstream parties and Islamist groups were generally poor and often hostile. The JKLF had also utilized Islamic formulations in its mobilization strategies and public discourse, using Islam and independence interchangeably. It demanded equal rights for everyone, however this had a distinct Islamic flavour as it sought to establish an Islamic democracy, protection of minority rights per Quran and Sunnah and an economy of Islamic socialism. The pro-separatist political practices at times deviated from their stated secular position.

- **Insurgency in Jammu and Kashmir**

In July 1988, the Jammu Kashmir Liberation Front (JKLF) began a separatist insurgency for secession of Kashmir from India. The group targeted a Kashmiri Hindu for the first time on 14 September 1989, when they killed Tika Lal Taploo, an advocate and a prominent leader of Bharatiya Janata Party in Jammu and Kashmir, in front of several eyewitnesses. This instilled fear in the Kashmiri Hindus especially as Taploo's killers were never caught which also emboldened the terrorists. The Hindus felt that they were not safe in the valley and could be targeted any time. The killings of Kashmiri Hindus, including many prominent ones, instilled more fear.

In order to undermine his political rival Farooq Abdullah who at that time was the Chief minister of Jammu and Kashmir, the Indian home minister Mufti Mohammad Sayeed convinced prime minister V.P. Singh to appoint Jagmohan as the governor of the state. Abdullah resented Jagmohan who had been appointed as the governor earlier in April 1984 as well and had recommended Abdullah's dismissal to Rajiv Gandhi in July 1984. Abdullah had earlier declared that he would resign if Jagmohan was made the Governor. However, the Central government went ahead and appointed him as Governor. In response, Abdullah resigned on 18 January 1990, and Jagmohan suggested the dissolution of the State Assembly.Most of the Kashmiri Hindus left Kashmir valley and moved to other parts of India, particularly to the refugee camps in Jammu region of the state.

- **Attack and threats**

1. On 14 September 1989, Tika Lal Taploo, who was a lawyer and a BJP member, was murdered by the JKLF in his home in Srinagar.
2. On 4 November, a judge Neelkanth Ganjoo, was shot dead near the Srinagar High court. He had sentenced Kashmiri separatist Maqbool Bhat to death in 1968.
3. In December, members of JKLF kidnapped Dr. Rubaiya Sayeed, daughter of the-then Union Minister Mufti Mohammad Sayeed,

demanding release of five militants, which was subsequently fulfilled.

4. On 4 January 1990, Srinagar-based newspaper Aftab released a message, threatening all Hindus to leave Kashmir immediately, sourcing it to the militant organization Hizbul Mujahideen.

On 14 April 1990, another Srinagar based newspaper Al-safa republished the same warning. The newspaper did not claim ownership of the statement and subsequently issued a clarification. Walls were pasted with posters with threatening messages to all Kashmiris to strictly follow Islamic rules which included abidance by the Islamic dress code, a prohibition on alcohol, cinemas, and video parlors and strict restrictions on women. Unknown masked men with Kalashnikovs forced people to reset their time to Pakistan Standard Time. Offices buildings, shops, and establishments were colored green as a sign of Islamic rule. Shops, factories, temples and homes of Kashmiri Hindus were burned or destroyed. Threatening posters were posted on doors of Hindus asking them to leave Kashmir immediately. During the middle of the night of 18 and 19 January, a blackout took place in the Kashmir Valley where electricity was cut except in mosques which broadcast divisive and inflammatory messages, asking for a purge of Kashmiri Hindus.

On 21 January, two days after Jagmohan took over as governor, the Gawkadal massacre took place in Srinagar, in which the Indian security forces had opened fire on protesters, leading to the death of at least 50 people, and likely over 100. These events led to chaos. Lawlessness took over the valley and the crowd with slogans and guns started roaming around the streets. News of violent incidents kept coming and many of the Hindus who survived the night saved their lives by traveling out of the valley.

On 25 January, the Rawalpora shooting incident took place, wherein four Indian Air Force personnel, Squadron Leader Ravi Khanna, Corporal D.B. Singh, Corporal Uday Shankar and Airman Azad Ahmad were killed and 10 other IAF personal were injured, while they were waiting at Rawalpora bus stand for their vehicle to pick them up in the morning. Altogether around 40 rounds were fired by the terrorists, apparently from 2 to 3 automatic weapons and one semi-automatic pistol. The Jammu and Kashmir Armed Police post located nearby, with 7 armed constables and one head constable, did not react. Jammu Kashmir Liberation Front (JKLF), with its leader Yasin Malik in particular, were allegedly involved in the killings. Incidents like these further expedited the exodus of Hindus from Kashmir.Several intelligence operatives were assassinated, over the course of January.

On 2 February, Satish Tikoo, a young Hindu social worker was murdered near his own house in Habba Kadal, Srinagar.On 13 February, Lassa Kaul, Station Director of Srinagar Doordarshan, was shot dead.On 29 April, Sarwanand Koul Premi, a veteran Kashmiri poet and his son were shot and hanged.On June 4, Girija Tickoo, a Kashmiri Hindu teacher was gang raped by terrorists, who ripped her abdomen and chopped her body into two pieces with a saw machine while she was still alive.

Many Kashmiri Pandit women were kidnapped, raped and murdered, throughout the time of exodus. The local organisation of Hindus in Kashmir, Kashmiri Pandit Sangharsh Samiti (KPSS), after carrying out a survey in 2008 and 2009, estimated 357 Hindus were killed in Kashmir in 1990.

- **Militancy in Kashmir**

Militancy in Kashmir increased after the exodus, and militants targeted properties of Kashmiri Hindus. Indian Home Ministry data records 1,406 Hindu civilian fatalities from 1991 to 2005. Jammu and Kashmir government stated that 219 members of the Hindu Pandit community had been killed between 1989 and 2004 and none thereafter.The Panun Kashmir organization has published a list of about 1,341 Hindus killed since 1990. The local organisation of Hindus in Kashmir, Kashmir Pandit Sangharsh Samiti (KPSS) after carrying out a survey in 2008 and 2009, said that 399 Kashmiri Hindus were killed by insurgents from 1990 to 2011 with 75% of them being killed during the first year of the Kashmiri insurgency, and that during the last 20 years, about 650 Hindus have been killed in the valley.

In response to the exodus, an organisation Panun Kashmir, a political group representing the Hindus who fled Kashmir, was formed. In late 1991, the organisation adopted the Margdarshan Resolution, which stated the need for a separate Union Territory in Kashmir division, Panun Kashmir. Panun Kashmir would serve as a homeland for Kashmiri Hindus and would resettle the displaced Kashmiri Pandits.In 2009 Oregon Legislative Assembly passed a resolution to recognise 14 September 2007, as Martyrs Day to acknowledge ethnic cleansing and campaigns of terror inflicted on non-Muslim minorities of Jammu and Kashmir by militants seeking to establish an Islamic state.

Kashmiri Hindus continue to fight for their return to the valley and many of them live as refugees. The exiled community had hoped to return after the situation improved. Most have not done so because the situation in the Valley remains unstable and they fear a risk to their lives. Most of them lost their properties after the exodus and many are unable to go back and sell them. Their status as displaced people has adversely harmed them in the realm of education. Many Hindu families could not afford to send their children to well regarded public schools. Furthermore, many Hindus faced institutional discrimination by predominantly Muslim state bureaucrats. As a result of the inadequate ad hoc schools and colleges formed in the refugee camps, it became harder for Hindu children to access education. They suffered in higher education as well, as they could not claim admission in PG colleges of Jammu university, while getting admitted in the institutes of Kashmir valley was out of question.

During the 2016 Kashmir unrest following the killing of Burhan Wani, transit camps housing Kashmir Hindus in Kashmir were attacked by mobs. About 200–300 Kashmiri Hindu employees fled the transit camps during night time on 12 July due to the attacks, and held protests against the government for attacks on their camp and demanded that all Kashmiri Hindus employees in Kashmir valley be evacuated immediately. Over 1300 government employees belonging to the community had fled the region during the unrest. Posters threatening the Hindus to leave Kashmir or be killed were also put up near transit camps in Pulwama allegedly by the militant organisation Lashkar-e-Toiba.

An organisation called Roots of Kashmir filed a petition in 2017 to reopen 215 cases of more than 700 alleged murders of Kashmiri Hindus, however the Supreme Court of India refused its plea. They have also demanded the creation of a "special crimes tribunal" to look into the ethnic cleansing and crimes committed. They also demanded a one time compensation for displaced Kashmiri Hindus who are not able to apply for government jobs.

The Indian Government has tried to rehabilitate the Hindus and the separatists have also invited the Hindus back to Kashmir. As of 2016, a total of 1,800 Kashmiri Hindu youths have returned to the Valley since the announcing of Rs. 1,168-crore package in 2008 by the UPA government. However, R.K. Bhat, president of Youth All India Kashmiri Samaj criticised the package to be a mere eyewash and claimed that most of the youths were living in cramped prefabricated sheds or in rented accommodation. He also said that 4,000 posts have been lying vacant since 2010 and alleged that the BJP government was repeating the same rhetoric and was not serious about helping them. The apathy on the part of the government and the sufferings of the Kashmiri Hindus have been highlighted in a play titled 'Kaash Kashmir'. Such efforts or claims have lacked political will as journalist Rahul Pandita writes in a memoir.

In an interview with NDTV on 19 January, Farooq Abdullah created controversy when he stated that the onus was on Kashmiri Hindus to come back themselves and nobody would beg them to do so. His comments were met with disagreement and criticism by Kashmiri Hindu authors Neeru Kaul, Siddhartha Gigoo, Congress MP Shashi Tharoor and Lt. General Syed Ata Hasnain. He also said that during his tenure as Chief Minister in 1996, he had asked them to return but they refused to do so. He reiterated his comments on 23 January and said that the time had come for them to return.

The issue of separate townships for Kashmiri Hindus has been a source of contention in the Kashmir valley, with Islamists, separatists, as well as mainstream political parties, all opposing it. Hizbul Mujahideen militant, Burhan Muzaffar Wani, had threatened of attacking the "Hindu composite townships" which were meant to be built for the rehabilitation of the non-Muslim community. In a 6-minute long video clip, Wani described the rehabilitation scheme as resembling Israeli designs. However, Burhan Wani welcomed the Kashmiri Hindus to return and promised to guard them. He also promised a safe Amarnath Yatra. Kashmiri Hindus residing in the Valley also mourned Burhan Wani's death. Burhan Wani's self-styled successor in the Hizbul Mujahideen, Zakir Rashid Bhat, also asked the Kashmiri Hindus to return and ensured them protection.

In 2010, the Government of Jammu and Kashmir noted that 808 Hindus families, comprising 3,445 people, were still living in the Valley and that financial and other incentives put in place to encourage others to return there had been unsuccessful. The employment package was also extended to Hindus who did not migrate out of the valley with an amendment to J&K Migrants (Special Drive) Recruitment Rules, 2009 in October 2017. The Indian Government has taken up the issue of education of the displaced students from Kashmir, and helped them get admissions in various Kendriya Vidyalayas and major educational institutions & universities across the country.

Some consider the now-abrogated Article 370 as a roadblock in the resettlement of Kashmiri Hindus as the Constitution of Jammu and Kashmir does not allow those living in India outside Jammu and Kashmir to freely settle in the state and become its citizens. Sanjay Tickoo, president of Kashmiri Pandit Sangharsh Samiti (KPSS), says that the 'Article 370' affair is different from the issue of exodus of Kashmiri Hindus and both should be dealt with separately. He remarks that, linking both the affairs is an "utterly insensitive way to deal with a highly sensitive and emotive issue"

THREE

INSURGENCY IN JAMMU AND KASHMIR

- **Insurgency in Jammu and Kashmir**

The insurgency in Jammu and Kashmir, also known as the Kashmir insurgency, is an ongoing separatist militant insurgency against the Indian administration in Jammu and Kashmir, a territory constituting the southwestern portion of the larger geographical region of Kashmir, which has been the subject of a territorial dispute between India and Pakistan since 1947.

Jammu and Kashmir, long a breeding ground of separatist ambitions, has been wracked by the insurgency since 1989. Although the failure of Indian governance and democracy lay at the root of the initial disaffection, Pakistan played an important role in converting the latter into a fully-developed armed insurgency. Some insurgent groups in Kashmir support complete independence, whereas others seek the region's accession to Pakistan.

More explicitly, the roots of the insurgency are tied to a dispute over local autonomy. Democratic development was limited in

Kashmir until the late 1970s, and by 1988, many of the democratic reforms provided by the Indian government had been reversed and non-violent channels for expressing discontent were limited, which caused a dramatic increase in support for insurgents advocating violent secession from India. In 1987, a disputed election held in the erstwhile state of Jammu and Kashmir created a catalyst for the insurgency when it resulted in some of the state's legislative assembly members forming armed insurgent groups. In July 1988, a series of demonstrations, strikes, and attacks on the Indian government effectively marked the beginning of the insurgency in Jammu and Kashmir, which escalated into the most severe security issue in India during the 1990s.

Pakistan, with whom India has fought three major wars over the Muslim-majority region, has officially claimed to be giving only its "moral and diplomatic" support to the separatist movement. The Pakistani Inter-Services Intelligence has been accused by both India and the international community of supporting and supplying arms as well as providing training to "mujahideen" militants in Jammu and Kashmir. In 2015, a former President of Pakistan, Pervez Musharraf, admitted that the Pakistani state had supported and trained insurgent groups in Kashmir throughout the 1990s. Several new militant groups with radical Islamist views emerged during this time and changed the ideological emphasis of the movement from that of plain separatism to Islamic fundamentalism. This occurred partly due to the influence of a large number of Muslim jihadist militants who began to enter the Indian-administered Kashmir Valley through Pakistani-controlled territory across the Line of Control following the end of the Soviet–Afghan War in the 1980s. India has repeatedly called on Pakistan to end its alleged "cross-border terrorism" in the region.

The conflict between militants and Indian security forces in Kashmir has led to a large number of casualties. many civilians have also died as a result of being targeted by various armed militant groups. According to official figures released in the Jammu and Kashmir assembly, there were 3,400 cases of disappearance and more than 47,000 people dead because of the conflict as of July 2009. Some human rights groups claim a higher figure of approximately 100,000 deaths since 1989.The insurgency has also forced the large-scale migration of non-Muslim minority populations—most notably that of Kashmiri Hindus—out of the Kashmir Valley.Since the revocation of the special status of Jammu and Kashmir in August 2019, the Indian military has intensified its counter-insurgency operations in the region.

- **Partition of India and First Kashmir War**

After independence from colonial rule India and Pakistan were engaged in a war over the princely state of Jammu and Kashmir. At the end of the war India controlled the southern portion of the princely state. While there were sporadic periods of violence there was no organised insurgency movement.During this period legislative elections in the state of Jammu and Kashmir were first held in 1951 and Sheikh Abdullah's secular party stood unopposed. He was an instrumental member in the accession of the state to India.

However, Sheikh Abdullah would fall in and out of favour with the central government and would often be dismissed only to be re-appointed later on. This was a time of political instability and power struggle in Jammu and Kashmir, and it went through several periods of president's rule by the Federal Government.

- **Kashmir 1982–2004**

The trend in total yearly civilian and security forces fatalities from insurgency-related violence over 25 years from 1988 to 2013.After Sheikh Abdullah's death, his son Farooq Abdullah took over as Chief Minister of Jammu and Kashmir. Farooq Abdullah eventually fell out of favour with the Central Government and the Prime Minister Indira Gandhi, who had his government toppled with the help of his brother-in-law G. M. Shah. GM Shah was the chief minister during the 1986 Anantnag Riots until he was removed and replaced by Farooq Abdullah. A year later, Abdullah reached an accord with the new Prime Minister Rajiv Gandhi and announced an alliance with the Indian National Congress for the elections of 1987. The elections were allegedly rigged in favour of Abdullah.

Most commentators state that this led to the rise of an armed insurgency movement composed, in part, of those who unfairly lost the elections. Pakistan supplied these groups with logistical support, arms, recruits and training.

In the second half of 1989 the alleged assassinations of the Indian spies and political collaborators by the Jammu Kashmir Liberation Front was intensified. Over six months more than a hundred officials were killed to paralyse government's administrative and intelligence apparatus. The daughter of then interior affairs minister, Mufti Mohammad Sayeed was kidnapped in December and four militants had to be released for her release. This event led to mass celebrations all over the valley. Farooq Abdullah resigned in January after the appointment of Jagmohan Malhotra as the Governor of Jammu and Kashmir. Subsequently, J&K was placed under Governor's Rule under Article 92 of state constitution.

Under JKLF's leadership on 21–23 January large scale protests were organised in the Kashmir Valley. As a response to this largely explosive situation paramilitary units of BSF and CRPF were called. These units were used by the government to combat Maoist insurgency and the North-Eastern insurgency. The challenge to them in this situation was not posed by armed insurgents but by the stone pelters. Their inexperience caused at least 50 casualties in Gawkadal massacre. In this incident the underground militant movement was transformed into a mass struggle. To curb the situation AFSPA (Armed Forces Special Powers Act) was imposed on Kashmir in September 1990 to suppress the insurgency by giving armed forces the powers to kill and arrest without warrant to maintain public order. During this time the dominant tactic involved killing of a prominent figure in a public gathering to push forces into action and the public prevented them from capturing these insurgents. This sprouting of sympathisers in Kashmir led to the hard-line approach of Indian army.

With JKLF at forefront large number of militant groups like Allah Tigers, People's League and Hizb-i-Islamia sprung up. Weapons were smuggled on a large scale from Pakistan. In Kashmir JKLF operated under the leadership of Ashfaq Majid Wani, Yasin Bhat, Hamid Shiekh and Javed Mir. To counter this growing pro-Pakistani sentiment in Kashmir, Indian media associated it exclusively with Pakistan.JKLF used distinctly Islamic themes to mobilise crowds and justify their use of violence. They sought to establish an Islamic democratic state where the rights of minorities would be protected according to Quran and Sunna and economy would be organised on the principles of Islamic socialism.

The Indian army has conducted various operations to control and eliminate insurgency in the region such as Operation Sarp Vinash, in which a multi-battalion offensive was launched against militants from groups like Lashkar-e-Taiba, Harkat-ul-Jihad-e-Islami, al-Badr and Jaish-e-Mohammed who had been constructing shelters in the Pir Panjal region of Jammu and Kashmir over several years. The subsequent operations led to the death of over 60 militants and uncovered the largest network of militant hideouts in the history of insurgency in Jammu and Kashmir covering 100 square kilometers.

- **Cultural changes**

Cinema houses were banned by some militant groups. Many militant organisations like Al baqr, People's league, Wahdat-e-Islam and Allah Tigers imposed restrictions like banning cigarettes, restrictions on Kashmiri girls.

- **2010 Kashmir unrest**

Beginning in 2004 Pakistan began to end its support for insurgents in Kashmir. This happened because militant groups linked to Kashmir twice tried to assassinate Pakistani President General Pervez Musharraf. His successor, Asif Ali Zardari has continued the policy, calling insurgents in Kashmir "terrorists", although it is unclear if Pakistan's intelligence agency, the Inter-Services Intelligence, thought to be the agency aiding and controlling the insurgency is following Pakistan's commitment to end support for the insurgency in Kashmir. Despite the change in the nature of the insurgency from a phenomenon supported by external forces to a primarily domestic-driven movement the Indian government has continued to send large numbers of troops to the Indian border. There have been widespread protests against the Indian army presence in Kashmir.

Once the most formidable face of Kashmir militancy, Hizbul Mujahideen is slowly fading away as its remaining commanders and cadres are being taken out on a regular interval by security forces. Some minor incidents of grenade throwing and sniper firing at security forces notwithstanding, the situation is under control and more or less peaceful. A record number of tourists including Amarnath pilgrims visited Kashmir during 2012. On 3 August 2012, a top Lashkar-e-Taiba militant commander, Abu Hanzulah involved in various attacks on civilians and security forces was killed in an encounter with security forces in a village in Kupwara district of north Kashmir.

According to Indian Army data quoted by Reuters, at least 70 young Kashmiris joined the insurgency in 2014, army records showed, with most joining the terrorist organization Lashkar-e-Taiba, which was responsible for carrying out the 2008 Mumbai attacks. Two of the new recruits have doctorates and eight were post graduates, the army data showed. According to BBC, despite a Pakistani ban on militant activity in Kashmir in 2006, its militants continue to attempt infiltration into Indian-administered Kashmir. These attempts were curtailed however when people living along the Line of Control which divides Indian and Pakistani Kashmir started to hold public protests against the activities of the insurgent groups.

In 2016, violence erupted in the aftermath of the killing of Hizbul Mujahideen militant Burhan Wani by security forces. Since then, militants belonging to the Jaish-e-Mohammed group carried out the 2016 Uri attack and the 2018 Sunjuwan attack. In February 2019, the Pulwama attack occurred, in which 40 CRPF personnel were killed by a Jaish-e-Mohammed suicide bomber. Border skirmishes between India and Pakistan occurred multiple times in 2013, 2014–2015, 2016–2018 and most notably in 2019. The latest skirmish ended with a ceasefire in February 2021.

In August 2019, the special status of Jammu and Kashmir was revoked, following which the Indian Army intensified its counter-insurgency operations. In June 2020, Doda district was declared militancy free while Tral was declared free from Hizbul Mujahideen militants. In July, a Kashmir police tweet from an official twitter handle said "no resident of #Srinagar district in terrorist ranks now". On 27 June 2021, a day after the successful completion of discussions between the Indian Prime Minister and Jammu and Kashmir political leaders, a drone based attack was reported at the technical area of Jammu Airport which is under the control of the IAF. In the first three months of 2022, there was a 100% increase in the number of Indian soldiers killed by Kashmiri militants compared to the same period in 2021.

- **1987 Jammu and Kashmir Legislative Assembly election**

Following the rise of Islamisation in the Kashmir valley, during the 1987 state elections, various Islamic anti-establishment groups including Jamaat-e-Islami Kashmir were organised under a single banner named Muslim United Front (MUF), that is largely current Hurriyat. MUF's election manifesto stressed the need for a solution to all outstanding issues according to Simla Agreement, work for Islamic unity and against political interference from the centre. Their slogan was wanting the law of the Quran in the Assembly. But the MUF won only four seats, even though it had polled 31% votes in the election. However, the elections were widely believed to be rigged, changing the course of politics in the state. The insurgency was sparked by the apparent rigging of state elections in 1987.

- **Human rights abuses in Jammu and Kashmir**

Indian troops entered the valley to quell the insurgency after it began. Some analysts have suggested that the number of Indian troops in Jammu and Kashmir is close to 600,000 although estimates vary and the government refuses to release official figures. The troops have been accused and held accountable for several humanitarian abuses and have engaged in mass extrajudicial killings, torture, rape and sexual abuse.

Indian security forces have been implicated in many reports for enforced disappearances of thousands of Kashmiris whereas the security forces deny having their information and/or custody. This is often in association with torture or extrajudicial killing. Human right activists estimate the number of disappeared to be over eight thousand, last seen in government detention. The disappeared are believed to be dumped in thousands of mass graves across Kashmir. A State Human Rights Commission inquiry in 2011, has confirmed there are thousands of bullet-ridden bodies buried in unmarked graves in Jammu and Kashmir. Of the 2730 bodies uncovered in 4 of the 14 districts, 574 bodies were identified as missing locals in contrast to the Indian governments insistence that all the graves belong to foreign militants.

Military forces in Jammu and Kashmir operate under impunity and emergency powers granted to them by the central government. These powers allow the military to curtail civil liberties, creating further support for the insurgency.The insurgents have also abused human rights, driving Kashmiri Pandits away from the Kashmir Valley, an action regarded as ethnic cleansing The government's inability to protect the people from both its own troops and the insurgency has further eroded support for the government.

Amnesty International accused security forces of exploiting the Armed Forces Special Powers Act (AFSPA) that enables them to "hold prisoners without trial". The group argues that the law, which allows security to detain individuals for as many as two years "without presenting charges, violating prisoners' human rights". The Army sources maintain that "any move to revoke AFSPA in Jammu and Kashmir would be detrimental to the security of the Valley and would provide a boost to the terrorists."

Former Indian Army Chief General V. K. Singh rejected the accusations that the action was not taken in the cases of human rights violations by Army personnel. On 24 October 2010, he has said that 104 Army personnel had been punished in Jammu and Kashmir in this regard, including 39 officers. He also said that 95% of the allegations of human rights abuses against Indian Army were proved to be false, of which he remarked, had apparently been made with the "ulterior motive of maligning the armed forces". However, according to Human Rights Watch, the military courts in India, in general, were proved to be incompetent to deal with cases of serious human rights abuses and were responsible in covering up evidence and protecting the involved officers. Amnesty International in its report in 2015, titled "Denied"-Failures in Accountability in Jammu and Kashmir, says, "...with respect to investigations, an inquiry that is conducted by the same authority accused of the crime raises serious questions about the independence and impartiality of those proceedings", adding that according to the international law, an independent authority that is not involved in the alleged violations has to investigate such crimes.These human rights violations are said to have contributed to the rise of resistance in Kashmir.

- **ISI's role**

The Pakistani Inter-Services Intelligence has encouraged and aided the Kashmir independence movement through an insurgency due to its dispute on the legitimacy of Indian rule in Kashmir, with the insurgency as an easy way to keep Indian troops distracted and cause international condemnation of India.

The Federal Bureau of Investigation (FBI), in their first ever open acknowledgement in 2011 in US Court, said that the Inter-Services Intelligence (ISI) sponsors and oversees separatist militant groups in Kashmir. In 2019, Prime Minister of Pakistan Imran Khan publicly discouraged Pakistani people from going to Kashmir to do a jihad. People who went to Kashmir will do an "injustice to the Kashmiri people". Most of the Pakistani militants who had crossed the border over the years and were caught by the Indian security forces were found to belong to the Punjab province of Pakistan.

- **Mujahideen victory**

After the Mujahideen victory in the Soviet–Afghan War, Mujahideen militants, under the Operation Tupac with the aid of Pakistan, slowly infiltrated Kashmir with the goal of spreading a radical Islamist ideology to wage Jihad against India in the region.

- **Religion**

The majority of the people of Jammu and Kashmir practise Islam. Indian-American journalist Asra Nomani states that while India itself is a secular state, Muslims are politically, culturally and economically marginalised when compared to Hindus in India as a whole. The government's decision to transfer 99 acres of forest land in near Amarnath in the Kashmir Valley to a Hindu organisation solidified this feeling and led to one of the largest protest rallies in Jammu and Kashmir.

- **Psychological**

Psychologist Waheeda Khan, explaining the rebellious nature of the Kashmiris, says that because of the tense situations in the valley from the 1990s, the generation gap between parents and young generations has increased. Young generations tend to blame their parents for failing to do anything about the political situation. So they start experimenting with their own aggressive ways to show their curbed feelings and would go against any authority. A prominent psychiatrist of the valley, Margoob, described that children/teenagers are much more vulnerable to passionate actions and reactions, since the young minds are yet to completely develop psychological mechanisms. When they assume that they are "pushed against the wall", they get controlled by the emotions without bothering about the consequences. Also young people easily identify themselves with the "group" rather than with their individual identities. It leads to psychological distress which causes antisocial behaviour and aggressive attitude. Often, this situation gets worsened by the availability of weapons and people becoming familiar to violence after having exposed to conflict for so long. Waheeda Khan remarks, the major concern is that generations of children who are experiencing long-term violence in their lives, may reach adulthood perceiving that violence is a fair means of solving ethnic, religious, or political differences.High unemployment and lack of economic opportunities in Kashmir are also said to have intensified the struggle.

- **Stone Pelting in Kashmir**

Since the 2008 protests and 2010 unrest, the turmoil has taken a new dimension when people, particularly youngsters of the Kashmir valley have started pelting stones on security forces to express their aggression and protest for the loss of freedom. In turn they get attacked by the armed personnel with pellets, rubber bullets, sling shots and tear gas shells. This leads to eye-injuries and several other kind of injuries to many people. Security forces also face injuries, and sometimes get beaten up during these events. According to Waheeda Khan, most of the 'stone-pelters' are school and college going students. Large number of these people get arrested during these events for allegedly resorting to stone pelting, after which some of them are also tortured. According to political activist Mannan Bukhari, Kashmiris made stone, an easily accessible and defenseless weapon, their weapon of choice for protest.

- **Kashmiri senior journalist Parvaiz Bukhari remarked**

The summer of 2010 witnessed a convulsion in the world's most militarized zone, the Indian-controlled part of Kashmir, an unprecedented and deadly civil unrest that is beginning to change a few things on the ground. Little known and relatively anonymous resistance activists emerged, organizing an unarmed agitation more fierce than the armed rebellion against Indian rule two decades earlier. And apparently aware of the post 9/11 world, young Kashmiris, children of the conflict, made stones and rocks a weapon of choice against government armed forces, side-stepping the tag of a terrorist movement linked with Pakistan. The unrest represents a conscious transition to an unarmed mass movement, one that poses a moral challenge to New Delhi's military domination over the region.

FOUR
THE KASHMIR

- **The Kashmir**

The history of Kashmir is intertwined with the history of the broader Indian subcontinent and the surrounding regions, comprising the areas of Central Asia, South Asia and East Asia. Historically, Kashmir referred to the Kashmir Valley. Today, it denotes a larger area that includes the Indian-administered union territories of Jammu and Kashmir and Ladakh, the Pakistan-administered territories of Azad Kashmir and Gilgit-Baltistan, and the Chinese-administered regions of Aksai Chin and the Trans-Karakoram Tract.

In the first half of the 1st millennium, the Kashmir region became an important centre of Hinduism and later—under the Mauryas and Kushanas—of Buddhism. Later in the ninth century, during the rule of the Karkota Dynasty, a native tradition of Shaivism arose. It flourished in the seven centuries of Hindu rule, continuing under the Utpala and the Lohara dynasties, ending in mid-14th century. Islamization in Kashmir began during the 13th century, accelerated under Muslim rule during the 14th and 15th centuries, and led to the eventual decline of the Kashmir Shaivism in Kashmir.

In 1339, Shah Mir became the first Muslim ruler of Kashmir, inaugurating the Shah Mir dynasty. For the next five centuries,

Muslim monarchs ruled Kashmir, including the Mughal Empire, who ruled from 1586 until 1751, and the Afghan Durrani Empire, which ruled from 1747 until 1819. That year, the Sikhs, under Ranjit Singh, annexed Kashmir. In 1846, after the Sikh defeat in the First Anglo-Sikh War, the Treaty of Lahore was signed and upon the purchase of the region from the British under the Treaty of Amritsar, the Raja of Jammu, Gulab Singh, became the new ruler of Kashmir. The rule of his descendants, under the paramountcy (or tutelage) of the British Crown, lasted until 1947, when the former princely state became a disputed territory, now administered by three countries: India, Pakistan, and the People's Republic of China.

According to folk etymology, the name "Kashmir" means "desiccated land". In the Rajatarangini, a history of Kashmir written by Kalhana in the mid-12th century, it is stated that the valley of Kashmir was formerly a lake. According to Hindu mythology, the lake was drained by the great rishi or sage, Kashyapa, son of Marichi, son of Brahma, by cutting the gap in the hills at Baramulla . When Kashmir had been drained, Kashyapa asked Brahmins to settle there. This is still the local tradition, and in the existing physical condition of the country, we may see some ground for the story which has taken this form. The name of Kashyapa is by history and tradition connected with the draining of the lake, and the chief town or collection of dwellings in the valley was called Kashyapa-pura, which has been identified with Kaspapyros of Hecataeus and Kaspatyros of Herodotus . Kashmir is also believed to be the country meant by Ptolemy's Kaspeiria. Cashmere is an archaic spelling of Kashmir, and in some countries it is still spelled this way.

Nilamata Purana contains accounts of Kashmir's early history. However, being a Puranic source, it has been argued that it suffers from a degree of inconsistency and unreliability. Kalhana's Rajatarangini , all the 8000 Sanskrit verses of which were completed by 1150 CE, chronicles the history of Kashmir's dynasties from earlier times to the 12th century. It relies upon traditional sources like Nilmata Purana, inscriptions, coins, monuments, and

Kalhana's personal observations borne out of political experiences of his family. Towards the end of the work mythical explanations give way to rational and critical analyses of dramatic events between 11th and 12th centuries, for which Kalhana is often credited as "India's first historian".

During the reign of Muslim kings in Kashmir, three supplements to Rajatarangini were written by Jonaraja (1411–1463 CE), Srivara, and Prajyabhatta and Suka, which end with Akbar's conquest of Kashmir in 1586 CE. The text was translated into Persian by Muslim scholars such as Nizam Uddin, Farishta, and Abul Fazl. Baharistan-i-Shahi and Haidar Mailk's Tarikh-i-Kashmir (completed in 1621 CE) are the most important texts on the history of Kashmir during the Sultanate period. Both the texts were written in Persian and used Rajatarangini and Persian histories as their sources.

This general view of the unexcavated Buddhist stupa near Baramulla, with two figures standing on the summit, and another at the base with measuring scales, was taken by John Burke in 1868. The stupa, which was later excavated, dates to 500 CE.

Earliest Neolithic sites in the flood plains of Kashmir valley are dated to c. 3000 BCE. Most important of these sites are the settlements at Burzahom, which had two Neolithic and one Megalithic phases. First phase (c. 2920 BCE) at Burzahom is marked by mud plastered pit dwellings, coarse pottery and stone tools. In the second phase, which lasted till c. 1700 BCE, houses were constructed on ground level and the dead were buried, sometimes with domesticated and wild animals. Hunting and fishing were the primary modes of subsistence though evidence of cultivation of wheat, barley, and lentils has also been found in both the phases. In the megalithic phase, massive circles were constructed and grey or black burnish replaced coarse red ware in pottery. During the later Vedic period, as kingdoms of the Vedic tribes expanded, the Uttara–Kurus settled in Kashmir.

- **Kanishka inaugurates Mahayana Buddhism in Kashmir**

In 326 BCE, Porus asked Abisares, the king of Kashmir, to aid him against Alexander the Great in the Battle of Hydaspes. After Porus lost the battle, Abhisares submitted to Alexander by sending him treasure and elephants.

During the reign of Ashoka (304–232 BCE), Kashmir became a part of the Maurya Empire and Buddhism was introduced in Kashmir. During this period, many stupas, some shrines dedicated to Shiva, and the city of Srinagari (Srinagar) were built. Kanishka (127–151 CE), an emperor of the Kushan dynasty, conquered Kashmir and established the new city of Kanishkapur. Buddhist tradition holds that Kanishka held the Fourth Buddhist council in Kashmir, in which celebrated scholars such as Ashvagosha, Nagarjuna and Vasumitra took part. By the fourth century, Kashmir became a seat of learning for both Buddhism and Hinduism. Kashmiri Buddhist missionaries helped spread Buddhism to Tibet and China and from the fifth century CE, pilgrims from these countries started visiting Kashmir. Kumārajīva (343–413 CE) was among the renowned Kashmiri scholars who traveled to China. He influenced the Chinese emperor Yao Xing and spearheaded translation of many Sanskrit works into Chinese at the Chang'an monastery.

- **Portable shrine with image of the Buddha, Jammu and Kashmir, 7-8th century**

The Alchon Huns under Toramana crossed over the Hindu Kush mountains and conquered large parts of western India including Kashmir. His son Mihirakula (c. 502–530 CE) led a military campaign to conquer all of North India. He was opposed by Baladitya in Magadha and eventually defeated by Yasodharman in Malwa. After the defeat, Mihirakula returned to Kashmir where he led a coup on the king. He then conquered of Gandhara where he committed many atrocities on Buddhists and destroyed their shrines. Influence of the Huns faded after Mihirakula's death.

- **Hindu Dynasties**

A succession of Hindu dynasties ruled over the region from the 7th-14th centuries. After the seventh century, significant developments took place in Kashmiri Hinduism. In the centuries that followed, Kashmir produced many poets, philosophers, and artists who contributed to Sanskrit literature and Hindu religion. Among notable scholars of this period was Vasugupta (c. 875–925 CE) who wrote the Shiva Sutras which laid the foundation for a monistic Shaiva system called Kashmir Shaivism. Dualistic interpretation of Shaiva scripture was defeated by Abhinavagupta (c. 975–1025 CE) who wrote many philosophical works on Kashmir Shaivism. Kashmir Shaivism was adopted by the common masses of Kashmir and strongly influenced Shaivism in Southern India.

Martand Sun Temple Central shrine, dedicated to the deity Surya. The temple complex was built by the third ruler of the Karkota dynasty, Lalitaditya Muktapida, in the 8th century CE. It is one of the largest temple complex on the Indian Subcontinent.

In the eighth century, the Karkota Empire established themselves as rulers of Kashmir. Kashmir grew as an imperial power under the Karkotas. Chandrapida of this dynasty was recognized by an imperial order of the Chinese emperor as the king of Kashmir. His successor Lalitaditya Muktapida lead a successful military campaign against the Tibetans. He then defeated Yashovarman of Kanyakubja and subsequently conquered eastern kingdoms of Magadha, Kamarupa, Gauda, and Kalinga. Lalitaditya extended his influence of Malwa and Gujarat and defeated Arabs at Sindh. After his demise, Kashmir's influence over other kingdoms declined and the dynasty ended in c. 855–856 CE.

The Utpala dynasty founded by Avantivarman followed the Karkotas. His successor Shankaravarman (885–902 CE) led a successful military campaign against Gurjaras in Punjab. Political instability in the 10th century made the royal body guards (Tantrins) very powerful in Kashmir. Under the Tantrins, civil administration collapsed and chaos reigned in Kashmir till they were defeated by Chakravarman. Queen Didda, who descended from the Hindu Shahis of Udabhandapura on her mother's side, took over as the ruler in second half of the 10th century. After her death in 1003 CE, the throne passed to the Lohara dynasty. Suhadeva, last king of the Lohara dynasty, fled Kashmir after Zulju (Dulacha), a Turkic–Mongol chief, led a savage raid on Kashmir. His wife, Queen Kota Rani ruled until 1339. She is often credited for the construction of a canal, named "Kutte Kol" after her, diverting the waters of the Jhelum to prevent frequent flooding in Srinagar.During the 11th century, Mahmud of Ghazni made two attempts to conquer Kashmir. However, both his campaigns failed because he could not take by siege the fortress at Lohkot.

- **Prelude and Kashmir Sultanate (1346–1580s)**

Historian Mohibbul Hasan states that the oppressive taxation, corruption, internecine fights and rise of feudal lords (Damaras) during the unpopular rule of the Lohara dynasty (1003–1320 CE) paved the way for foreign invasions of Kashmir. Rinchana was a Tibetan Buddhist refugee in Kashmir, who had established himself as the ruler after Zulju. Rinchana's conversion to Islam is a subject of Kashmiri folklore. He was persuaded to accept Islam by his minister Shah Mir, probably for political reasons. Islam had penetrated into countries outside Kashmir and in absence of the support from Hindus, who were in a majority, Rinchana needed the support of the Kashmiri Muslims. Shah Mir's coup on Rinchana's successor secured Muslim rule and the rule of his dynasty in Kashmir.

In the 14th century, Islam gradually became the dominant religion in Kashmir. With the fall of Kashmir, a premier center of Sanskrit literary creativity, Sanskrit literature there disappeared. 397–398 Islamic preacher Sheikh Nooruddin Noorani, who is traditionally revered by Hindus as Nund Rishi, combined elements of Kashmir Shaivism with Sufi mysticism in his discourses. The Sultans between 1354 and 1470 CE were tolerant of other religions with the exception of Sultan Sikandar (1389–1413 CE). Sultan Sikandar imposed taxes on non–Muslims, forced conversions to

Islam, and earned the title But–Shikan for destroying idols. Sultan Zain-ul-Abidin (c. 1420–1470 CE) invited artists and craftsmen from Central Asia and Persia to train local artists in Kashmir. Under his rule the arts of wood carving, papier-mâché , shawl and carpet weaving prospered. For a brief period in the 1470s, states of Jammu, Poonch and Rajauri which paid tributes to Kashmir revolted against the Sultan Hajji Khan. However, they were subjugated by his son Hasan Khan who took over as ruler in 1472 CE. By the mid 16th century, Hindu influence in the courts and role of the Hindu priests had declined as Muslim missionaries immigrated into Kashmir from Central Asia and Persia, and Persian replaced Sanskrit as the official language. Around the same period, the nobility of Chaks had become powerful enough to unseat the Shah Mir dynasty.

Silver sasnu of the Kashmir Sultan Shams al-Din Shah II (ruled 1537–38). During the Sultanate period, the Kashmir sultans issued silver and copper coins. The silver coins were square and followed a weight standard unique to Kashmir of between 6 and 7 gm. This coin weighs 6.16 gm.

Mughal general Mirza Muhammad Haidar Dughlat, a member of ruling family in Kashgar, invaded Kashmir in c. 1540 CE on behalf of emperor Humayun. Persecution of Shias, Shafi'is and Sufis and instigation by Suri kings led to a revolt which overthrew Dughlat's rule in Kashmir.

- **Mughals (1580s–1750s)**

Kashmir did not witness direct Mughal rule till the reign of Mughal badshah (emperor) Akbar the Great, who took control of Kashmir and added it to his Kabul Subah in 1586. Shah Jahan carved it out as a separate subah , with seat at Srinagar. During successive Mughal emperors many celebrated gardens, mosques and palaces were constructed. Religious intolerance and discriminatory taxation reappeared when Mughal emperor Aurangzeb ascended to the throne in 1658 CE. After his death, the influence of the Mughal Empire declined.

Shalimar Bagh in Srinagar; the Mughals built several charbagh-style gardens all over the Kashmir valley. In 1700 CE, a servant of a wealthy Kashmir merchant brought Mo-i Muqqadas (the hair of the Prophet), a relic of Muhammad, to the valley. The relic was housed in the Hazratbal Shrine on the banks of Dal Lake. Nadir Shah's invasion of India in 1738 CE further weakened Mughal control over Kashmir.

- **Durrani Empire (1752–1819)**

Taking advantage of the declining Mughal Empire, the Afghan Durrani Empire under Ahmad Shah Durrani took control of Kashmir in 1752. In the mid-1750s the Afghan-appointed governor of Kashmir, Sukh Jiwan Mal, rebelled against the Durrani Empire before being defeated in 1762. After Mal's defeat, the Durrani engaged in the oppression of the remaining Hindu population through forced conversions, killings, and forced labor. Repression by the Durrani extended to all classes, regardless of religion, and a heavy tax burden was levied on the Kashmiri populace.

A number of Afghan governors administrated the region on behalf of the Durrani Empire. During the Durrani rule in Kashmir, income from the region constituted a large part of the Durrani Empire's revenue. The empire controlled Kashmir until 1819, after which the region was annexed by the Sikh Empire.

- **Sikh rule (1820–1846)**

After four centuries of Muslim rule, Kashmir fell to the conquering armies of the Sikhs under Ranjit Singh of Punjab after the Battle of Shopian in 1819. As the Kashmiris had suffered under the Afghans, they initially welcomed the new Sikh rulers. However, the Sikh governors turned out to be hard taskmasters, and Sikh rule was generally considered oppressive, protected perhaps by the remoteness of Kashmir from the capital of the Sikh Empire in Lahore. The Sikhs enacted a number of anti-Muslim laws, which included handing out death sentences for cow slaughter, closing down the Jamia Masjid in Srinagar, and banning the azaan, the public Muslim call to prayer.

Kashmir had also now begun to attract European visitors, several of whom wrote of the abject poverty of the vast Muslim peasantry and of the exorbitant taxes under the Sikhs. High taxes, according to some contemporary accounts, had depopulated large tracts of the countryside, allowing only one-sixteenth of the cultivable land to be cultivated. However, after a famine in 1832, the Sikhs reduced the land tax to half the produce of the land and also began to offer interest-free loans to farmers; Kashmir became the second highest revenue earner for the Sikh empire. During this time Kashmiri shawls became known worldwide, attracting many buyers especially in the west.

Earlier, in 1780, after the death of Ranjit Deo, the kingdom of Jammu was also captured by the Sikhs and made a tributary. Ranjit Deo's grandnephew, Gulab Singh, subsequently sought service at the court of Ranjit Singh, distinguished himself in later campaigns and got appointed as the Raja of Jammu in 1820. With the help of his officer, Zorawar Singh, Gulab Singh soon captured for the Sikhs the lands of Ladakh and Baltistan. 10th century Boniar temple in 1876, cleared during the Dogra rule. Best preserved Kashmir temple.

In 1845, the First Anglo-Sikh War broke out, and Gulab Singh "contrived to hold himself aloof till the battle of Sobraon (1846), when he appeared as a useful mediator and the trusted advisor of Sir Henry Lawrence. Two treaties were concluded. By the first the State of Lahore (West Punjab) handed over to the British, as equivalent for (rupees) ten million of indemnity, the hill countries between Beas and Indus; by the second the British made over to Gulab Singh for (Rupees) 7.5 million all the hilly or mountainous country situated to the east of Indus and west of Ravi" (the Vale of Kashmir).

The Treaty of Amritsar freed Gulab Singh from obligations towards the Sikhs and made him the Maharajah of Jammu and Kashmir. The Dogras' loyalty came in handy to the British during the revolt of 1857 which challenged British rule in India. Dogras refused to provide sanctuary to mutineers, allowed English women and children to seek asylum in Kashmir and sent Kashmiri troops to fight on behalf of the British. British in return rewarded them by securing the succession of Dogra rule in Kashmir. Soon after Gulab Singh's death in 1857,his son, Ranbir Singh, added the emirates of Hunza, Gilgit and Nagar to the kingdom.

The Princely State of Kashmir and Jammu was constituted between 1820 and 1858 and was "somewhat artificial in composition and it did not develop a fully coherent identity, partly as a result of its disparate origins and partly as a result of the autocratic rule which it experienced on the fringes of Empire." It combined disparate regions, religions, and ethnicities: to the east, Ladakh was ethnically and culturally Tibetan and its inhabitants practised Buddhism; to the south, Jammu had a mixed population of Hindus, Muslims and Sikhs; in the heavily populated central Kashmir valley, the population was overwhelmingly Sunni Muslim, however, there was also a small but influential Hindu minority, the Kashmiri brahmins or pandits; to the northeast, sparsely populated Baltistan had a population ethnically related to Ladakh, but which practised Shi'a Islam; to the north, also sparsely populated, Gilgit Agency, was an area of diverse, mostly Shi'a groups; and, to the west, Punch was Muslim, but of different ethnicity than the Kashmir valley.

Despite being in a majority the Muslims were made to suffer severe oppression under Hindu rule in the form of high taxes, unpaid forced labor and discriminatory laws. Many Kashmiri Muslims migrated from the Valley to Punjab due to famine and policies of Dogra rulers. The Muslim peasantry was vast, impoverished and ruled by a Hindu elite. The Muslim peasants lacked education, awareness of rights and were chronically in debt to landlords and moneylenders, and did not organize politically until the 1930s.

- **1947**

Ranbir Singh's grandson Hari Singh, who had ascended the throne of Kashmir in 1925, was the reigning monarch in 1947 at the conclusion of British rule of the subcontinent and the subsequent partition of the British Indian Empire into the newly independent Dominion of India and Dominion of Pakistan. An internal revolt began in the Poonch region against oppressive taxation by the Maharaja. In August, Maharaja's forces fired upon demonstrations in favour of Kashmir joining Pakistan, burned whole villages and massacred innocent people. The Poonch rebels declared an independent government of "Azad" Kashmir on 24 October. Rulers of Princely States were encouraged to accede their States to either Dominion – India or Pakistan, taking into account factors such as geographical contiguity and the wishes of their people. In 1947, Kashmir's population was "77% Muslim and 20% Hindu". To postpone making a hurried decision, the Maharaja signed a standstill agreement with Pakistan, which ensured continuity of trade, travel, communication, and similar services between the two. Such an agreement was pending with India.

Following huge riots in Jammu, in October 1947, Pashtuns from Pakistan's North-West Frontier Province recruited by the Poonch rebels, invaded Kashmir, along with the Poonch rebels, allegedly incensed by the atrocities against fellow Muslims in Poonch and Jammu. The tribesmen engaged in looting and killing along the way. The ostensible aim of the guerilla campaign was to frighten Hari Singh into submission. Instead the Maharaja appealed to the Government of India for assistance, and the Governor-General Lord Mountbatten agreed on the condition that the ruler accede to India.

Once the Maharaja signed the Instrument of Accession, Indian soldiers entered Kashmir and drove the Pakistani-sponsored irregulars from all but a small section of the state. India accepted the accession, regarding it provisional until such time as the will of the people can be ascertained. Kashmir leader Sheikh Abdullah endorsed the accession as ad hoc which would be ultimately decided by the people of the State. He was appointed the head of the emergency administration by the Maharaja. The Pakistani government immediately contested the accession, suggesting that it was fraudulent, that the Maharaja acted under duress and that he had no right to sign an agreement with India when the standstill agreement with Pakistan was still in force.

- **Post-1947**

In early 1948, India sought a resolution of the Kashmir Conflict at the United Nations. Following the set-up of the United Nations Commission for India and Pakistan (UNCIP), the UN Security Council passed Resolution 47 on 21 April 1948. The UN mission insisted that the opinion of people of J&K must be ascertained. The then Indian Prime Minister is reported to have himself urged U.N. to poll Kashmir and on the basis of results Kashmir's accession will be decided. However, India insisted that no referendum could occur until all of the state had been cleared of irregulars.

On 5 January 1949, UNCIP (United Nations Commission for India and Pakistan) resolution stated that the question of the accession of the State of Jammu and Kashmir to India or Pakistan will be decided through a free and impartial plebiscite. As per the 1948 and 1949 UNCIP Resolutions, both countries accepted the principle, that Pakistan secures the withdrawal of Pakistani intruders followed by withdrawal of Pakistani and Indian forces, as a basis for the formulation of a Truce agreement whose details are to be arrived in future, followed by a plebiscite; However, both countries failed to arrive at a Truce agreement due to differences in interpretation of the procedure for and extent of demilitarisation one of them being whether the Azad Kashmiri army of Pakistan is to be disbanded during the truce stage or the plebiscite stage.

In the last days of 1948, a ceasefire was agreed under UN auspices; however, since the plebiscite demanded by the UN was never conducted, relations between India and Pakistan soured, and eventually led to three more wars over Kashmir in 1965, 1971 and 1999. India has control of about half the area of the former princely state of Jammu and Kashmir; Pakistan controls a third of the region, governing it as Gilgit–Baltistan and Azad Kashmir. According to Encyclopædia Britannica, "Although there was a clear Muslim majority in Kashmir before the 1947 partition and its economic, cultural, and geographic contiguity with the Muslim-majority area of the Punjab (in Pakistan) could be convincingly demonstrated, the political developments during and after the partition resulted in a division of the region. Pakistan was left with territory that, although basically Muslim in character, was thinly populated, relatively inaccessible, and economically underdeveloped. The largest Muslim group, situated in the Valley of Kashmir and estimated to number more than half the population of the entire region, lay in Indian-administered territory, with its former outlets via the Jhelum valley route blocked."

- **Cease-fire line between India and Pakistan after the 1947**

The UN Security Council on 20 January 1948 passed Resolution 39 establishing a special commission to investigate the conflict. Subsequent to the commission's recommendation the Security Council, ordered in its Resolution 47, passed on 21 April 1948 that the invading Pakistani army retreat from Jammu & Kashmir and that the accession of Kashmir to either India or Pakistan be determined in accordance with a plebiscite to be supervised by the UN. In a string of subsequent resolutions the Security Council took notice of the continuing failure by India to hold the plebiscite. However, no punitive action against India could be taken by the Security Council because its resolution, requiring India to hold a Plebiscite, was non-binding. Moreover, the Pakistani army never left the part of the Kashmir, they managed to keep occupied at the end of the 1947 war. They were required by the Security Council resolution 47 to remove all armed personnels from the Azad Kashmir before holding the plebiscite.

The eastern region of the erstwhile princely state of Kashmir has also been beset with a boundary dispute. In the late 19th- and early 20th centuries, although some boundary agreements were signed between Great Britain, Afghanistan and Russia over the northern borders of Kashmir, China never accepted these agreements, and the official Chinese position did not change with the communist revolution in 1949. By the mid-1950s the Chinese army had entered the north-east portion of Ladakh. "By 1956–57 they had completed a military road through the Aksai Chin area to provide better communication between Xinjiang and western Tibet. India's belated discovery of this road led to border clashes between the two countries that culminated in the Sino-Indian war of October 1962."China has occupied Aksai Chin since 1962 and, in addition, an adjoining region, the Trans-Karakoram Tract was ceded by Pakistan to China in 1965.

In 1949, the Indian government obliged Hari Singh to leave Jammu and Kashmir and yield the government to Sheikh Abdullah, the leader of a popular political party, the National Conference Party. Since then, a bitter enmity has been developed between India and Pakistan and three wars have taken place between them over Kashmir. The growing dispute over Kashmir and the consistent failure of democracy also led to the rise of Kashmir nationalism and militancy in the state.

In 1986, the Anantnag riots broke out after the CM Gul Shah ordered the construction of a mosque at the site of a Hindu Temple in Jammu and Gul Shah made an incendiary speech. Hindu-Muslim riots (a reaction to the opening of Babri Masjid to Hindu worshippers) were a national event, taking place in seven other states as well. Following the 1987 Jammu and Kashmir Legislative Assembly election that were widely perceived to have been rigged, disgruntled Kashmiri youth such as the so-called 'HAJY group' – Abdul Hamid Shaikh, Ashfaq Majid Wani, Javed Ahmed Mir and Mohammed Yasin Malik – joined the Jammu and Kashmir Liberation Front(JKLF) as an alternative to the ineffective democratic setup that was prevalent in Kashmir. This led to gain in the momentum of the popular insurgency in the Kashmir Valley. The year 1989 saw the intensification of conflict in Jammu and Kashmir as Mujahadeens from Afghanistan slowly infiltrated the region following the end of the Soviet–Afghan War the same year. Pakistan provided arms and training to both indigenous and foreign militants in Kashmir, thus adding fuel to the smouldering fire of discontent in the valley.

In August 2019, the Government of India repealed the special status accorded to Jammu and Kashmir under Article 370 of the Indian constitution in 2019, and the Parliament of India passed the Jammu and Kashmir Reorganisation Act, which contained provisions to dissolve the state and reorganise it into two union territories – Jammu and Kashmir in the west and Ladakh in the east. These changes came into effect from 31 October 2019.

Among the Muslims of the Kashmir province within the princely state, four divisions were recorded: "Shaikhs, Saiyids, Mughals, and Pathans. The Shaikhs, who are by far the most numerous, are the descendants of Hindus, but have retained none of the caste rules of their forefathers. They have clan names known as krams ..." It was recorded that these kram names included "Tantre", "Shaikh", "Bat", "Mantu", "Ganai", "Dar", "Damar", "Lon", etc. The Saiyids, it was recorded, "could be divided into those who follow the profession of religion and those who have taken to agriculture and other pursuits. Their kram name is 'Mir.' While a Saiyid retains his saintly profession Mir is a prefix; if he has taken to agriculture, Mir is an affix to his name." The Mughals who were not numerous were recorded to have kram names like "Mir" (a corruption of "Mirza"), "Beg", "Bandi", "Bach" and "Ashaye". Finally, it was recorded that the Pathans "who are more numerous than the Mughals, ... are found chiefly in the south-west of the valley, where Pathan colonies have from time to time been founded.

The most interesting of these colonies is that of Kuki-Khel Afridis at Dranghaihama, who retain all the old customs and speak Pashtu." Among the main tribes of Muslims in the princely state are the Butts, Dar, Lone, Jat, Gujjar, Rajput, Sudhan and Khatri. A small number of Butts, Dar and Lone use the title Khawaja and the Khatri use the title Shaikh the Gujjar use the title of Chaudhary. All these tribes are indigenous of the princely state which converted to Islam from Hinduism during its arrival in region.Among the Hindus of Jammu province, who numbered 626,177 (or 90.87% of the Hindu population of the princely state), the most important castes recorded in the census were "Brahmans (186,000), the Rajputs (167,000), the Khattris (48,000) and the Thakkars (93,000)."

FIVE

2019 PULWAMA ATTACK

- **Terrorist attacks in India (since 2001)**

The 2019 Pulwama attack occurred on 14 February 2019, when a convoy of vehicles carrying Indian security personnel on the Jammu–Srinagar National Highway was attacked by a vehicle-borne suicide bomber at Lethapora in the Pulwama district of the erstwhile state of Jammu and Kashmir. The attack killed 40 Indian Central Reserve Police Force (CRPF) personnel as well as the perpetrator—Adil Ahmad Dar—who was a local Kashmiri youth from the Pulwama district. The responsibility for the attack was claimed by the Pakistan-based Islamist terrorist group, Jaish-e-Mohammed. India blamed neighbouring Pakistan for the attack, while the latter condemned the attack and denied having any connections to it. The attack dealt a severe blow to India–Pakistan relations, consequently resulting in the 2019 India–Pakistan military standoff. Subsequently, Indian investigations identified 19 accused. By August 2021, the main accused along with six others had been killed, and seven had been arrested.

Kashmir is a disputed territory, claimed both by India and Pakistan with both countries administering part of the territory.

Pakistan has sought to gain control of Indian-administered Kashmir. An insurgency began to proliferate in Indian-administered Kashmir in the late 1980s. Pakistan provided the insurgency with material support. Since 1989, about 70,000 people have been killed in the uprising and the Indian crackdown. According to Time, unrest in Kashmir grew in 2016 after India killed a popular militant leader, Burhan Wani. A rising number of young locals from Indian administered Kashmir have joined the militancy. Many sources state that the majority of militants in Kashmir are now local, not foreign. In 2018 alone, the death toll included 260 militants, 160 civilians and 150 government forces.

Since 2015, Pakistan-based militants in Kashmir have increasingly taken to high-profile suicide attacks against the Indian security forces. In July 2015, three gunmen attacked a bus, and police station in Gurdaspur. Early in 2016, four to six gunmen attacked the Pathankot Air Force Station. In February and June 2016, the militants killed nine and eight security personnel respectively in Pampore. In September 2016, four assailants attacked an Indian Army brigade headquarters in Uri killing 19 soldiers. On 31 December 2017, the Commando Training Centre at Lethpora was also attacked by militants killing five security personnel. These attacks took place in the vicinity of the Jammu Srinagar National Highway.

- **On 14 February 2019**

On 14 February 2019, a convoy of 78 vehicles transporting more than 2,500 Central Reserve Police Force (CRPF) personnel from Jammu to Srinagar was travelling on National Highway 44. The convoy had left Jammu around 03:30 IST and was carrying a large number of personnel due to the highway having been shut down for two days prior. The convoy was scheduled to reach its destination before sunset.

At Lethpora near Awantipora, around 15:15 IST, a bus carrying security personnel was rammed by a car carrying explosives. It caused a blast which killed 40 CRPF personnel of the 76th Battalion and injured many others. The injured were moved to the army base hospital in Srinagar.

Pakistan-based militant group Jaish-e-Mohammed claimed responsibility for the attack. They also released a video of the assailant Adil Ahmad Dar, a 22-year-old from Kakapora who had joined the group a year earlier. Dar's family had last seen him in March 2018, when he left his house on a bicycle one day and never returned. Pakistan denied any involvement, though Jaish-e-Mohammed's leader, Masood Azhar, is known to operate in the country.It is the deadliest terror attack on India's state security personnel in Kashmir since 1989.

The perpetrator was identified as Adil Ahmad Dar, a 22-year old from Kakapora. According to Dar's parents, Dar became radicalized after he was beaten by Indian police. Between September 2016 and March 2018, Adil Dar was reportedly arrested six times by Indian authorities. However, each time he was released without any charges.

- **Investigation**

The National Investigation Agency (NIA) dispatched a 12-member team to probe the attack, working with the Jammu and Kashmir Police.Initial investigations suggested the car was carrying more than 300 kilograms (660 lb) of explosives, including 80 kilograms (180 lb) of RDX, a high explosive, and ammonium nitrate. Lt Gen Hooda said that the explosives might have been stolen from a construction site. He initially said that it was not possible that they were smuggled from across the border, but later said that he could not rule it out.

National Investigation Agency was able to establish and confirm the identity of suicide bomber as DNA samples from "meagre fragments of the car" used in suicide attack matched with Adil Ahmad Dar's father. However, even after a year of investigation, NIA was unable to trace the source of explosives. The charge-sheet filed by the NIA in August 2020 named 19 accused.

- **Candle light march organised in Mehsana, Gujarat**

State funerals of security personnel killed in the attack were held in their respective native places. The government of Punjab announced ex gratia compensation of 12 lakh (US15,000) each to the families of the killed security personnel from the state and a government job to the next of kin. India revoked Pakistan's most favoured nation status. The customs duty on all Pakistani goods imported to India were raised to 200%. The government of India urged the Financial Action Task Force on Money Laundering (FATF) to put Pakistan on the blacklist. The FATF decided to keep it on the 'grey list' and gave Pakistan time till October 2019 to comply with the 27 conditions it had laid down in June 2018, when it was put on the 'grey list', with an attending caveat. If Pakistan failed to comply, it would be added to the blacklist. On 17 February, the state administration revoked security provisions for separatist leaders.

Protests, bandhs and candle light marches were held across India. There were violent protests in Jammu resulting in a curfew being imposed starting 14 February. The Indian community in the United Kingdom held protests outside the Pakistan High Commission in London. A delegation of Indian doctors cancelled their visit to Pakistan for the 13th Association of Anaesthesiologists Congress, organised by the South Asian Association for Regional Cooperation, in Lahore on 7 March. Indian broadcaster DSport said it would no longer broadcast Pakistan Super League cricket matches. The All Indian Cine Workers Association announced a ban on Pakistani actors and artists in the Indian film industry, and stated that strong action would be taken on any organisation violating it. The Indian Film and Television Directors Association also announced a ban on Pakistani artists in films and music produced in India; the president of the organisation threatened to "vandalise" the sets of any Indian film production with Pakistani artists.

On 20 February 2019, Pakistani prisoner Shakarullah, who was serving a life term in India's Jaipur Central Jail under Unlawful Activities (Prevention) Act, was stabbed and beaten to death by four other inmates. India claimed that Shakarullah was allegedly killed in a brawl among the inmates over television volume. Pakistan claimed that he was killed in retaliation of the Pulwama incident.

- **Gunfight with the militants**

Following intelligence inputs, in the early morning hours of 18 February, a joint team comprising 55 Rashtriya Rifles, CRPF and Special Operations Group of India killed two terrorists and two supporters in an anti-terrorism encounter operation in the ensuing manhunt for the perpetrators in Pulwama. One of them, Abdul Rasheed Ghazi alias Kamran, was identified as a Pakistani national and was considered the mastermind of the attack and a commander of the terrorist group Jaish-e-Muhammad (JeM). In addition, local JeM recruit Hilal Ahmed, along with two sympathisers who housed Ghazi and Ahmed to evade capture, were also shot dead in the encounter. Four security personnel were killed in the gunfight.

- **Anti-Kashmiri backlash**

Kashmiri students living in other parts of India faced a backlash after the attack, including violence and harassment, and eviction from their homes. In response, many Indians offered to house Kashmiris who may have been evicted.

It was reported that number of Kashmiris fleeing from the rest of India had reached "hundreds". Jammu and Kashmir Students Organisation reported that 97% of Kashmiri students in Dehradun had been evacuated. Two Indian colleges in Dehradun announced that no new Kashmiri students will receive admission. One of those colleges, Alpine College, suspended its dean, who is a Kashmiri, after some groups called for him to be fired.

Tathagata Roy, the governor of the Indian state Meghalaya, tweeted support for a boycott of "everything Kashmiri". Union Minister Ravi Shankar Prasad disagreed with this view. A Kashmiri merchant was beaten in Kolkata; the attack was condemned by West Bengal chief minister Mamata Banerjee.Kashmir police chief Dilbagh Singh said they had asked affected states to protect students." Former Jammu and Kashmir chief minister Omar Abdullah met with Rajnath Singh seeking assistance.

- **2019 Balakot airstrike**

On 26 February, twelve Mirage 2000 jets of the Indian Air Force crossed the Line of Control and dropped bombs into Balakot, Pakistan. India claimed that it attacked a Jaish-e-Mohammed training camp and killed a large number of terrorists, reported to be between 300 and 350. Pakistan claimed that they quickly scrambled jets to intercept the IAF jets, who dropped their payloads to quickly return over the Line of Control

- **India-Pakistan standoff**

On 27 February, Pakistan Air Force conducted an airstrike into Jammu and Kashmir in retaliation for the Indian airstrike the day before. Both Pakistan and India agreed that no damage was caused by Pakistan's airstrike. However, in an ensuing dogfight between Indian and Pakistani jets, an Indian MiG-21 was shot down over Pakistan and its pilot captured. Pakistan released the pilot on 1 March.

- **Pakistan arrests suspects**

On 5 March, Pakistan arrested 44 members of various groups, including the Jaish-e-Muhammad. Some of those arrested had been named by India in a dossier it gave to Pakistan in the aftermath of the Pulwama attack. Pakistan said those arrested will be held for at least 14 days, and if India provided further evidence they would be prosecuted. Among those arrested were relatives of JeM leader Masood Azhar, including his son Hamad Azhar and his brother Abdul Rauf.

- **Arrests and operations in India**

By August 2021, Indian security forces had killed seven of the accused, including Saifullah, while seven had been arrested.

- **India and Pakistan**

Indian Prime Minister Narendra Modi condemned the attack and expressed solidarity with the victims and their families. Union Home Minister Rajnath Singh assured that a strong response will be given to the terror attack. India blamed Pakistan for the attack. BBC News has said that the involvement of the Jaish-e-Mohammed in the bombing "directly links" Pakistan to the attack, while also pointing out that Jaish-e-Mohammed had attacked Pakistani military targets in the past. It is widely accepted among security analysts that Jaish-e-Mohammed is the creation of Pakistan's Inter-Services Intelligence. Pakistan banned the group in 2002, but it has resurfaced under different names and retains ISI's support. The New York Times questioned the nature of the link to Pakistan, pointing out that the bomber came from Indian-administered Kashmir and the explosives may also have been locally procured.The Indian Finance Minister Arun Jaitley has said that India would completely isolate Pakistan in the diplomatic community.

Pakistan denied the allegation of a link to the attack, and Pakistani foreign minister Shah Mahmood Qureshi condemned the bombing. Fawad Chaudhry, Pakistan's federal information minister, said that Pakistan was taking action against Jaish-e-Muhammad and that Pakistan would be able to assist India in taking action against terrorist groups. The Nation, a Pakistani newspaper, called the assailant a "freedom fighter" who eliminated members of an "occupying force". Pakistan and India both recalled their ambassadors for "consultations" in a tit-for-tat move.

On 19 February 2019, Pakistani Prime Minister Imran Khan said that providing safe haven to terrorists was not in Pakistan's interest. He asked for proof of Pakistani involvement and warned India that any military response would be met with retaliation. Indian Ministry of External Affairs responded by criticising him for not condemning the attack and not offering any condolences for the victims. It said that claims by Adil Ahmad Dar and Pakistan-based Jaish-e-Mohammed was sufficient proof.

It said that promises of investigation was unconvincing due to a lack of progress in Mumbai and Pathankot attack investigations. In response to Indian criticism, the newspaper Dawn pointed out that Pakistani Foreign Minister Qureshi had expressed sympathies with the victims soon after the attack.Following the attack on the Indian territory, the producers of the Indian Hindi films, including Notebook, Kabir Singh and Satellite Shankar, decided not to release the films in Pakistan.Former Indian cricket players and Board of Control for Cricket in India (BCCI) called for the boycott on the 2019 World Cup group match fixture between India and Pakistan with raising concerns on banning Pakistan cricket team from playing in the 2019 Cricket World Cup tournament. However, after conducting a press meet in Dubai, the International Cricket Council (ICC) rejected BCCI's statement regarding banning Pakistan from the World Cup and assured that the scheduled match will go ahead as planned despite the ongoing standoff between the two nations.

On 8 March 2019, the India national cricket team wore camouflage military caps in tribute to the CRPF personnel killed in the attack during the third ODI against Australia at Ranchi. The players also donated their match fees to the National Defence Fund. The Pakistan Cricket Board wrote to the ICC to protest the gesture. The ICC stated that BCCI had asked for, and received, permission to wear the caps.

- **International community**

The United States condemned the attack and added it would work with India in counterterrorism efforts. It asked Pakistan to stop sheltering terrorists and urged it to cooperate with the investigation and punish those responsible. Pakistan said it was ready to cooperate with such an investigation. A statement from the US Department of State noted that Pakistan-based Jaish-e-Mohammed had claimed responsibility for the attack. Bangladesh, Bhutan, China, France, Hungary, Israel, Maldives, Nepal, Russia, Saudi Arabia, Singapore, Sri Lanka, Turkey, the United Arab Emirates, and the United Kingdom condemned the attack, as did the United Nations Secretary-General.China and Turkey also defended Pakistan's efforts to fight terrorism. China placed a temporary block on a UN Security Council resolution following the attack, which was backed by all other permanent members of the council, to designate JeM leader Masood Azhar as a global terrorist.

Iran's Deputy Foreign Minister Abbas Araghchi met with India's External Affairs Minister Sushma Swaraj and referring to both the 2019 Pulwama attack and the 2019 Khash–Zahedan suicide bombing, he stated that Iran and India would work together to prevent future attacks.

The Indian cricket team paid tribute to the 40 soldiers killed in the Pulwama attack by wearing the camouflage caps instead of the usual sky blue team India cap, during the third One Day International match with Australia in Ranchi. Pakistan objected to this gesture and Pakistani Information Minister Fawad Chaudhry and Foreign Minister Shah Mahmood Qureshi called the International Cricket Council (ICC) to ban the Indian team for allegedly mixing cricket with politics. After a complaint from the Pakistani Cricket Board, The ICC clarified that the Indian team had requested and was granted permission to wear the camouflage caps as a part of fundraising drive and to pay tribute to the soldiers killed in the attack

SIX

2016 Uri Attack

The 2016 Uri attack was carried out on 18 September by four Jaish-e-Mohammed insurgents from Pakistan against an Indian Army brigade headquarters near the town of Uri in the erstwhile Indian state of Jammu and Kashmir. 19 Indian soldiers were killed in the attack, and 19–30 others were injured. It was reported by the BBC as having been "the deadliest attack on security forces in Kashmir in two decades". Jaish-e-Mohammed, a Pakistan-based Jihadist organization , was involved in the planning and execution of the attack. At the time it was carried out, the Kashmir Valley was experiencing high levels of violent unrest.

Since 2015, the insurgents had increasingly taken to high-profile fidayeen attacks (suicide attacks) against the Indian security forces: in July 2015, three insurgents attacked a bus and police station in Gurdaspur and earlier in 2016, 4–6 terrorists attacked the Pathankot Air Force Station. Indian authorities blamed Jaish-e-Mohammad for the latter attack.Also, since 8 July 2016, the Indian state of Jammu and Kashmir has been undergoing continuous unrest following the killing of Burhan Wani, the leader and local commander of the Hizb-ul-Mujahideen. The killing sparked violent protests against the Indian government in the valley, leading to the protests being described as the "largest anti-India protests" against Indian rule in recent years.

- **Attack**

At around 5:30 a.m. on 18 September, four insurgents attacked an Indian Army brigade headquarters in Uri, near the Line of Control in a pre-dawn ambush. They were said to have lobbed 17 grenades in three minutes. As a rear administrative base camp with tents caught fire, 17 army personnel were killed during the attack. An additional 19–30 soldiers were reported to have been injured. A gun battle ensued lasting six hours, during which all the four individuals were killed. Combing operations continued to flush out additional terrorists thought to be alive.

Most of the Indian soldiers had suffered casualties and subsequently those who died were from the 10th battalion, Dogra Regiment (10 Dogra) and 6th battalion, Bihar Regiment (6 Bihar). One of the injured soldiers succumbed to his injuries on 19 September at RR Hospital in New Delhi, followed by another soldier on 24 September, bringing the death toll to 19.

The casualties were primarily believed to have occurred as a result of non-fire retardant transition tents. This was the time of a troops shift, whereby troops from 6 Bihar were replacing troops from 10 Dogra. The incoming troops were housed in tents, which are normally avoided in sensitive areas around the LoC like Uri. The insurgents snuck into the camp breaching heavy security and seemed to know exactly where to strike. Seven of the personnel killed were support staff, including cooks and barbers.

On 19 September, Home Minister Rajnath Singh, Defence Minister Manohar Parrikar, Chief of the Army Staff Dalbir Singh, National Security Advisor Ajit Doval and other officials of the Home and Defence ministries met to review the security situation in Kashmir, particularly in areas along the Line of Control. The National Investigation Agency filed a first information report regarding the attack and took over the investigation from Jammu and Kashmir Police on 20 September.

Pakistan International Airlines cancelled flights to some parts of Kashmir on 21 September in the aftermath of the attack. Security around the army installation in Uri was intensified following the attack, while soldiers on both the Indian and Pakistani side of Line of Control were placed on high alert.

- **Postponement of SAARC summit**

In the wake of the attack, India cancelled its participation in the 19th SAARC summit to be held in November in Islamabad, Pakistan. The Ministry of External Affairs issued a statement, saying, "India has conveyed to current SAARC Chair Nepal that increasing cross-border terrorist attacks in the region and growing interference in the internal affairs of Member States by one country have created an environment that is not conducive to the successful holding of the 19th SAARC Summit in Islamabad in November 2016." "In the prevailing circumstances, the Government of India is unable to participate in the proposed Summit in Islamabad", the statement said.

On India withdrawing from the scheduled SAARC summit in Islamabad, Pakistan's Foreign Office termed the withdrawal "unfortunate", and posted a rejoinder stating: "As for the excuse used by India, the world knows that it is India that has been perpetrating and financing terrorism in Pakistan." The statement included a reference to Indian national Kulbhushan Jadhav, detained by Pakistan for espionage, and accused India of violating international laws by interfering inside Pakistan.

Later, Afghanistan, Bangladesh and Bhutan also withdrew from the summit. On 30 September 2016, Pakistan stated that the summit scheduled for 9 and 10 November in Islamabad would be held on an alternative date.

- **2016 Indian Line of Control strike**

On 28 September, eleven days after the attack, the Indian Army conducted retaliatory surgical strikes on alleged launch-pads used by terrorists in Pakistan administered Kashmir. Indian Director

General of Military Operations (DGMO) Lt Gen Ranbir Singh said that it had made a preemptive strike against "terrorist teams" who were preparing to "carry out infiltration and conduct terrorist strikes inside Jammu and Kashmir and in various metros in other states". The Economist while citing Indian reports, reported that Indian commandos crossed the Line of Control and struck at the safe houses, allegedly killing approximately 150 Pakistan-sponsored terrorists.

- **Bilateral boycott**

Following the uproar after the Uri attack, Indian Motion Picture Producers Association (IMPPA) decided to ban all Pakistani actors, actresses and technicians working in India till the situation returns to normal. Bollywood artists were divided towards the ban with some justifying it while some questioning its benefits. Indian TV entertainment channel Zindagi announced discontinuation of airing Pakistani TV shows on the channel. The Pakistani government responded in October with a blanket ban on all Indian television and radio programming in Pakistan.

The Board of Control for Cricket in India (BCCI), the national governing body for cricket in India, ruled out the possibility of reviving bilateral cricket ties with Pakistan in the near future. BCCI also asked the International Cricket Council (ICC) to not group Indian and Pakistan cricket teams together in international tournaments, keeping in mind border tensions between the two countries. Badminton Association of India, the governing body for badminton in India, decided to boycott the Pakistan International Series scheduled to be held in Islamabad in October, as an act of "solidarity" with the government's diplomatic offensive against Pakistan.

An initial investigation into the attack indicated that there were several procedural lapses at the camp. According to the standard security procedures, any tall grass and bushes around vital security installations should be trimmed. However, this procedure was not followed by the Uri camp which might have allowed insurgents to sneak into the camp undetected using the tall grass and bushes around the perimeter. In addition, the probe also indicated that two manned guard posts failed to detect the intrusion because the coordination between them might have been poor. It also indicated that the terrorists had infiltrated the Indian territory through Haji Pir Pass on the intervening night of 16–17 September and stayed in Sukhdar village which is located at a vantage point that allows an unhindered view of the layout of the camp as well as movement of the personnel in it.

The Director General Military Operations (DGMO) Lt. Gen. Ranbir Singh briefing the media on the terrorist attack at Army Camp, in Uri, a day after the attacks, on September 19, 2016.

The Director General of military operations, Lieutenant-General Ranbir Singh, said that there was evidence that the individuals involved in the attack belonged to Jaish-e-Mohammad. He established a hotline contact with his Pakistani counterpart and conveyed India's serious concern on the issue. Singh also stated that the militants used incendiary ammunition to set fire to the tents.

- **The Indian Ministry of External Affairs said**

In the recent incidents, we have recovered a number of items that include GPS from the bodies of terrorists with coordinates that indicate the point and time of infiltration across the LoC and the subsequent route to the terror attack site; grenades with Pakistani markings; communication matrix sheets; communication equipment; and other stores made in Pakistan, including food, medicines and clothes.

Former Pakistani General Pervez Musharraf said the weapons that India reported as used by militants, and reported to have Pakistani markings, could be procured anywhere in the world, not just in Pakistan. Musharraf further said since many American weapons had inadvertently fallen into the hands of the Taliban, it is possible for Pakistani weapons to have been acquired by the perpetrators without Pakistani involvement.

On 25 September, the Indian Army said that two Pakistani nationals from Pakistan administered Kashmir were arrested by the Border Security Force in the Uri sector. They were said to have been recruited by Jaish-e-Muhammad two years ago for the purpose of acting as guides to infiltrating groups in the Uri sector. These guides themselves did not have a role in the Uri attack. They were being questioned for gathering intelligence about infiltration attempts. Pakistan denied these allegations. On 26 February 2017, India's National Investigative Agency (NIA) decided to file a closure report after failing to find any evidence against the two men whom they accused of facilitating the Uri army base attack.

On 25 October 2016, the Indian media reported that street "posters" in Gujranwala, Pakistan, attributed to Lashkar-e-Taiba (LeT) claimed responsibility for the Uri attack. The posters claimed that one of LeT's fighters Mohammad Anas, code-named Abu Saraqa, died in the Uri attack, and there would be a funeral prayer followed by a speech by the LeT chief Hafiz Saeed on 25 October. The poster also claimed death of 17 Indian soldiers in Uri attack. After the images of the poster circulated on the Internet, the organisation claimed that it was a hoax. Abbas Nasir, the former editor of Dawn, confirmed the report about the posters on Twitter but stated that the funeral prayers have been postponed.

Thank You

Thank You For Reading This Book And Shared This Book To Friends As Birthday Gift Have A Wonderfull Day .

Printed by Libri Plureos GmbH in Hamburg,
Germany